16 EXTRAORDINARY
YOUNG AMERICANS

NANCY LOBB

WALCH PUBLISHING®

Photo Credits

Benjamin West	Dover Pictorial Archive
Phillis Wheatley	The Bettmann Archive
Maria Mitchell	Corbis-Bettmann
Allen Jay	Friends Historical Library of Swarthmore College
Mary Jane Dilworth	Used by permission, Utah State Historical Society
Orion Howe	Massachusetts Commandery Military Order of the Loyal Legion and the U.S. Army Military History Institute
Shirley Temple	©1988 AP/WORLD WIDE PHOTOS
Melba Pattillo	UPI/Corbis-Bettmann
S.E. Hinton	Courtesy of Beverly Hinton
Midori	©1997 AP/WORLD WIDE PHOTOS
Ryan White	©1988 AP/WORLD WIDE PHOTOS
Trevor Ferrell	©1986 AP/WORLD WIDE PHOTOS
Samantha Smith	©1983 AP/WORLD WIDE PHOTOS
Oscar De La Hoya	©1997 AP/WORLD WIDE PHOTOS
Tiger Woods	©1995 AP/WORLD WIDE PHOTOS
Jason Gaes	©1992 AP/WORLD WIDE PHOTOS

1   2   3   4   5   6   7   8   9   10

ISBN 0-8251-3796-9

Copyright © 1998
J. Weston Walch, Publisher
P. O. Box 658 • Portland, Maine 04104-0658

Printed in the United States of America

Contents

Introduction

> Throughout our history we have profited by the daring of our young people, by their bold adventurousness, by their hunger for new horizons, by their willingness to make sacrifices and to seek something without knowing what they sought.
>
> —*John Gardner, President of the Carnegie Corporation, 1957*

Young Americans today get a lot of bad press. News stories point out examples of school dropouts or youth in trouble with the law. Teenagers have been called lazy, spoiled, and immoral. But the vast, unsung majority of American teens are going to school, making good grades, and contributing to their communities. Throughout U.S. history, many young people have shown courage, dedication, and intelligence far beyond their years. The 16 American young people profiled in this book are outstanding examples. The lives of these American young people have made a difference in the story of the United States.

In this book you will read the stories of 16 teenagers who made extraordinary contributions to our nation while in their teens (or even younger). The stories include:

- Benjamin West, the first artist of Colonial America

- Phillis Wheatley, the first African-American poet

- Maria Mitchell, an astronomer who discovered a comets

- Allen Jay, a "conductor" on the Underground Railroad

- Mary Jane Dilworth, the first school teacher of Utah

- Orion Howe, a heroic Civil War drummer boy

- Shirley Temple, a child star

- Melba Pattillo, a member of the Little Rock Nine

- S.E. Hinton, the author of *The Outsiders*

- Midori, a professional violinist

- Ryan White, a spokesperson for people living with AIDS

- Trevor Ferrell, an activist for the homeless

- Samantha Smith, a goodwill ambassador to the Soviet Union

- Oscar De La Hoya, a boxing champion

- Tiger Woods, a professional golfer

- Jason Gaes, a cancer survivor who wrote a children's book about cancer

The motto on the Great Seal of the United States reads E PLURIBUS UNUM. That is Latin for "out of many, one." The United States is made up of people of different races, creeds, genders—and ages. Throughout her history, America's youngest citizens have shown great creativity, courage, and compassion. We must not forget the important contributions of American youth, both in the past and the present. I hope you will enjoy reading about these 16 American young people who have made a difference.

—Nancy Lobb

Benjamin West
Artist

> No other artist of any land at any time has ever so completely influenced and dominated the art of his country.
>
> —*Albert Rosenthal (20th-century painter, speaking of Benjamin West)*

Benjamin West

Benjamin West is known as the Father of American Painting. He was the first important artist to emerge from Colonial America. Nearly every major painter of his time studied with him. His work led to three major new schools, or styles, of art.

Born on October 19, 1738, Benjamin West was the youngest of 10 children. At Benjamin's birth, a Quaker preacher foretold that Benjamin was bound for greatness. Benjamin proved this prophecy true at a very early age. By the time he reached his teens, Benjamin was known as an artist in all the American colonies.

The West family lived 10 miles outside Philadelphia. Benjamin's father was an innkeeper. The inn was an exciting place for a boy to grow up. A steady flow of travelers meant plenty of interesting happenings. Families new to America passed through, speaking different languages. There was always work to be done at the crowded inn. Benjamin was kept busy doing chores.

Benjamin's parents were Quaker. Yet they did not follow all the strict Quaker beliefs. None of their 10 children was listed on the church rolls. The rolls list all the official members of the church.

One day when Benjamin was six, his married sister came to visit with her new baby. Benjamin's mother and sister went for a walk. Benjamin was asked to watch the sleeping baby.

While it slept, the baby suddenly smiled. A strange feeling came over Benjamin. He picked up a pen and piece of paper lying on a nearby table. He drew a picture of the child.

Just then, Benjamin heard his mother returning. Afraid, he tried to hide the drawing. But his mother knew he'd been up to something.

He was afraid she would be angry when she saw the drawing. Quakers frowned on drawings, especially pictures of people. Drawings were thought to be sinful. There were no paintings or pictures anywhere in Quaker homes. Benjamin himself had never even seen a drawing. Neither had his parents or his neighbors.

Benjamin's mother looked at his drawing for a long time. It looked just like the baby. She was so amazed at Benjamin's skill that she did not scold him.

A few of the Quakers condemned Benjamin for drawing. But because of the preacher's prophecy, most accepted his talent as a gift from God. Benjamin was allowed to keep drawing. Word traveled fast about the small boy and his ability to draw what he saw.

A number of Native Americans lived nearby. Sometimes they stopped at the inn. Benjamin showed them his drawings of birds and flowers. The Native Americans asked why none of his drawings were in color. Benjamin answered that he had only black ink. The Indians then showed him how to make the red and yellow paints which they themselves used. His mother then showed him how to make blue, using indigo dye. Benjamin then had the three primary colors.

One day a visitor remarked that Benjamin needed a paint brush. Benjamin did not know what a brush was. In those days, a brush was made from camel's hair fastened to a quill. (A quill is the hollow shaft of a feather.) There were no camels nearby. Benjamin decided that cat hair would work instead. He cut a chunk of fur from the family cat to make a brush.

The brush did not last long. Soon Benjamin needed more fur. Before long, the cat began to look raggedy. His father remarked that the cat must be sick. Benjamin was forced to confess what he had been doing.

The cat's lot was about to improve. In 1744, one of Benjamin's cousins, Mr. Pennington, came to visit at the inn. He was impressed with Benjamin's drawings. When he went home, he sent Benjamin a box of paints, some brushes, and canvases. He also sent six engravings by an artist. These were the first pictures and first real paint and brushes Benjamin had ever seen.

Benjamin was thrilled with the gift. For several days he secretly stayed home from school. He hid in the attic with his paints. There he made a painting which combined parts of two of the engravings. He continued skipping school until the day when the teacher asked his mother where Benjamin had been.

When Benjamin was nine years old, Mr. Pennington returned for another visit. He was amazed at what Benjamin had done with his gift. He asked Benjamin's parents if he might take the boy back to Philadelphia for a visit.

In the city, Mr. Pennington gave Benjamin materials for creating oil paintings. The boy began a landscape painting. William Williams, a well-known painter, came to see him work. He was impressed with Benjamin. Williams asked if the boy knew of the famous painters in Europe. The boy answered that the only great people he had read about were those in the Bible.

Williams gave Benjamin two classic books on painting to take home. The books were long and dull. Benjamin could read only a little, having been a poor student. But he later said, "Those two books were my companions by day, and under my pillow at night." While it is likely that he understood very little of the books, they were his introduction to classical paintings. The nine-year-old boy decided then that he would be an artist.

One day Benjamin spied some wide boards at a carpenter's shop near his home. He asked if he could have six boards to draw on. On each board, he drew a portrait. These he sold to a neighbor, who paid him one dollar apiece for them. (This was a large sum at the time.) This was the first money he had earned from his art.

By the time he was 12, Benjamin had sold many more pictures. By 16, he did a good business painting portraits of his neighbors. At 17 he was asked to do two portraits in Lancaster, two days' ride away. He ended up staying in the town for a year. During this time, he painted portraits of eight of the town's leading citizens.

One of these citizens was William Henry, a gunsmith. He had hired Benjamin to paint a portrait of him with his new wife. Henry knew a lot about art in Europe.

He told Benjamin that painting portraits was a job unworthy of his talents. He felt that Benjamin should paint great moments from history. He suggested that Benjamin paint about the death of Socrates. Benjamin did so. He finished "The Death of Socrates" in 1756 at the age of 18.

This picture was important because it was his first "history painting." Benjamin would later make this new style of painting popular in Europe.

Benjamin returned to Philadelphia. At that time, it was a city of 15,000 people. It was the center of wealth and culture in America. Benjamin fit in well with its high society. He was in much demand as a portrait painter. But he had no luck winning a wife. None of the mothers felt that an artist was a good match for their daughters. (He was unlikely to be able to support a wife well.) To one young woman he was courting, Benjamin gave a miniature portrait of himself. This is the picture shown at the beginning of this story.

In 1758, Benjamin went to New York City to paint some portraits. He knew he could charge higher fees there. He hoped to save enough money to go to Italy. Italy was then the art capital of the world. He wanted to study with master painters there.

A merchant gave him free passage on a cargo ship. Soon Benjamin was on his way. He studied three years in Italy with a famous painter. In 1763 he went to London for a visit. He ended up staying there for the rest of his life.

Famous painters and wealthy Englishmen took to the young American. King George III became a close friend. In 1772 Benjamin was appointed the "historical painter to the king." He was also named a charter member of the Royal Academy of Arts.

As part of his job, Benjamin painted historical scenes on huge canvases. He was the first artist to paint people in the style of clothing they actually wore. At that time artists always showed people dressed in Greek and Roman clothing, no matter what time period they lived in. It was a bold move for Benjamin to paint people the way they really looked.

Benjamin West shared his talent with young artists. His studio was always full of young people wanting art lessons. He taught a number of young American artists who later became great artists in America.

Benjamin West died in London in 1820 at the age of 82. He had painted over 400 paintings for King George III. He was a beloved artist on two continents. In Europe he was known as the founder of a new school of historical painting. In America he was remembered as the young Quaker boy from Colonial America who became a world-famous artist.

Remembering the Facts

1. Where and when was Benjamin born?

2. What prophecy was made at his birth?

3. What was the subject of Benjamin's first drawing?

4. Why did Benjamin think his mother would be angry when she saw his drawing?

5. How did Benjamin make his paintbrushes?

6. How did William Williams's gift help Benjamin?

7. Why was "The Death of Socrates" an important painting?

8. Why did Benjamin dream of going to Italy?

9. What position did Benjamin gain in 1772?

10. How were Benjamin's historical paintings different from others of the time?

Understanding the Story

11. If Benjamin's parents had been strict Quakers, what effect do you think that would have had on his artistic career?

12. There were very few Colonial artists in America when Benjamin West was a boy. Why do you think that was so?

Getting the Main Idea

Benjamin lived his adult life in England. Why do you think he is known today as the Father of American Painting?

Applying What You've Learned

A person may be born with a gift for painting or drawing. What role do you think formal training might have in developing such a gift?

Phillis Wheatley
Poet

In 1985, the governor of Massachusetts declared February 1 to be Phillis Wheatley Day. Phillis Wheatley was the first African American to publish a book. She wrote this book of poems while she was in her teens.

Phillis Wheatley

Phillis was born around 1753 in West Africa. When she was about seven years old, she was kidnapped by slave traders. With many others, she was packed into the hold of the slave ship *Phillis*. The long voyage to America began.

Conditions on the trip were grim. The slaves were beaten. They were given little to eat. They had no room to move about. There was no fresh air. Many slaves died during the trip. The others were weak and sick by the time they arrived in Boston.

A slave sale was held in Boston. Mrs. Susannah Wheatley, wife of a Boston merchant, was looking for a young woman to do house-work. Phillis was not at all what she had in mind. The girl was thin and dirty, and only seven years old. She would not be good for much work.

But something about the girl's face interested Mrs. Wheatley. She bought the girl and took her home. She did not know the girl's name. So, she named her "Phillis" after the ship that brought her. Phillis was also given the family's last name, Wheatley.

Mrs. Wheatley had 18-year-old twins—Mary and Nathaniel. Mary was given the job of teaching Phillis. Phillis learned to do some simple household tasks. But Mary also taught her to speak English and to read the Bible.

It quickly became clear that Phillis was no ordinary child. Sixteen months after coming to America she could read English well. She could understand the Bible verses she read. Mary began teaching Phillis poetry. Nathaniel taught her Latin.

It was most unusual in those days for a slave to be educated. For one thing, girls of all races in the 18th century were usually denied "book learning." They were expected to become wives and mothers. Also, most people at that time did not believe black people could learn as well as white people. Teaching a black person to read was against the law in some states. In others it was discouraged. A black person who could read might not want to remain a slave. Most families would have forbidden Phillis to study. But not the Wheatleys.

Phillis began writing poetry at the age of 12. The Wheatley family encouraged her. They gave her paper, ink, and a quill pen. They gave her candles so she could write in her room at night. Many mornings she would surprise them with a new poem she had written. The poems were stunning. Phillis's use of language was amazing.

The Wheatley family saw that Phillis was remarkable. Her gifts were rare. They helped and encouraged Phillis to develop her talent. In fact, Mrs. Wheatley was to spend the rest of her days promoting Phillis's career.

Mrs. Wheatley was proud of "her Phillis." She invited important Bostonians to her home to meet Phillis. Phillis was invited into other wealthy homes to read her poetry. She became a sought-after guest at parties. The upper class of Boston all knew and loved Phillis.

But Phillis was never really one of them. As a black female she would never be accepted as a social equal. Yet her masters thought she was too good for the company of other slaves. She would remain trapped between the two worlds all her life.

During Phillis's teen years, America was moving toward the Revolutionary War. In 1768 British troops landed in Boston. Phillis wrote about this in a widely read poem. It was called, "On the Arrival of the Ships of War, and the Landing of the Troops." She was 15 years old.

In 1770, Phillis went to a series of sermons by George White-field. He was a powerful speaker who greatly inspired all who heard him. He taught that people of all colors are equal in God's sight. When he died a month later, Phillis wrote an elegy to honor him. (An elegy is a poem of sorrow about a death.)

The poem was published in the form of a pamphlet. Because Whitefield had been so popular, the poem was widely read. Phillis became famous throughout the colonies. The pamphlet gave some facts about its author. It read: "By Phillis, a Servant Girl of 17 Years of Age, belonging to Mr. J. Wheatley, of Boston:-and has been but nine years in this Country from Africa."

Mrs. Susannah Wheatley decided now was the time to publish a collection of Phillis's poems. She sent Phillis's poems to a publisher in London. He was impressed with the poems. But he did not believe a black slave had written them. Finally, he agreed to publish them if it could be proved that Phillis had written the poems herself.

Mrs. Wheatley had no trouble getting 18 well-known Bostonians to sign a paper stating that Phillis was the poet. Among the signers were John Hancock and Thomas Hutchinson, governor of Massachusetts. The signatures are found in the front of the book on a page marked "To the Publick."

In those days, a book sold better if it was dedicated to a famous person. Phillis dedicated her book to the Countess of Huntingdon in England. Huntingdon was rich and well-known. Her support of Phillis's book meant the book would sell well.

Huntingdon wanted a portrait of Phillis in the front of the book. So, Phillis sat for a portrait. It is believed to have been painted by Scipio Moorhead, a black slave. It is the only portrait of Phillis known to exist. (It is the one shown at the beginning of this story.)

When Phillis was 19, Nathaniel Wheatley planned to sail to London on business. Mrs. Wheatley decided to send Phillis with him. Countess Huntingdon spread the word of the young poet's upcoming visit. When Phillis arrived, she found she was famous, even though her book had not yet been published.

Phillis Wheatley began a social whirl. She was invited to the finest homes. Noble people and wealthy people all loved Phillis. She was the talk of the town. Not only that, the English treated Phillis as an equal.

But her visit was cut short just a month later with bad news. Susannah Wheatley was dying. She wished for Phillis to return home. Phillis felt that she had no choice but to do so.

In September 1773, the first copies of Phillis's book were published. It was titled *Poems on Various Subjects, Religious and Moral.* The publisher called it "one of the greatest instances of pure, unassisted genius that the world ever produced."

English reviewers praised the book. But they spoke against the Wheatleys for keeping Phillis a slave. Soon after Phillis returned from England, the Wheatleys set her free.

Phillis's life began to change rapidly. In March 1774, Susannah Wheatley died. In May of that year, 300 copies of Phillis's book finally reached the colonies. They sold quickly. They had arrived just in time. A month later, the British blocked all ships from entering Boston harbor. The Revolutionary War was under way.

Phillis was impressed with General George Washington. So she wrote a poem honoring him in 1775. She called him "great chief, with virtue on thy side." Washington liked the poem so much, he invited Phillis to come for a meeting. The two talked in private for 30 minutes. It was a memory Phillis would treasure the rest of her life.

Also that year she wrote a poem called "Reply." In it, she praised the beauty of Africa and its "native grace." This is the first time known in American literature in which an African American praises his or her African heritage.

But it was wartime. Times were hard. People were losing their jobs and homes. No one had time or money to help a young poet. Phillis could not earn a living with her poetry. She was unable to get a second book of poems published.

She decided to get married. The next year she had a child. The baby died soon after birth. Then her husband's business failed. He was thrown into debtors' prison. A second child died. Phillis was alone and without money.

The war ended in 1783. The following year, Phillis wrote her last poem. It was called "Liberty and Peace." The poem celebrates the birth of the new nation. It begins with the words: "Lo! Freedom comes."

Sadly, Phillis never lived to see the poem in print. By this time she was living in a rundown home for penniless black people. She died on December 5, 1784, soon after giving birth to her third child. She was 31 years old.

In an unfortunate sign of her times, Phillis's remarkable life and achievements sadly were not recognized in her death. She was buried in an unmarked grave.

Phillis Wheatley was a black woman at a time when black people were slaves and women were hidden at home. Yet she has an honored place in American history as the first African-American poet.

Phillis Wheatley overcame many obstacles in her short life- time. Her poetry is a testament to the strength of the human spirit. Her poems call out for freedom and justice. Her inspiring words tell of an enslaved people's yearning for freedom. Phillis herself was only free in her imagination. As she wrote:

> Imagination! who can sing thy force?
> Or who describe the swiftness of thy course?
> Soaring through air to find the bright abode,
> The (imperial) palace of the thundering God,
> We on the pinions can surpass the wind,
> And leave the rolling universe behind.

For many years after her death, Phillis's poetry was forgotten. Then, during the mid-1800's, people called abolitionists began talking about her poetry. (These people were working to abolish slavery.) They pointed out that black people were talented in many fields, just as any people. Therefore, it was wrong to keep them in slavery.

Nearly a century after writing her final poem, Phillis Wheatley inspired a generation of people trying to end a shameful chapter of American history. The slave who became a poet took her rightful place in the history of American literature.

Remembering the Facts

1. Where and when was Phillis born?

2. How was Phillis educated?

3. How did Phillis's poetry become known in Boston?

4. Why did the London publisher refuse at first to publish Phillis's poetry?

5. How did the English learn about Phillis's poetry?

6. What was the title of Phillis's only book?

7. How did Phillis meet General Washington?

8. Why did Phillis end her days in poverty?

Understanding the Story

9. In what ways do you think the Wheatley family was unusual in the way it treated Phillis?

10. In what ways did the Revolutionary War affect Phillis's life?

Getting the Main Idea

Why do you think Phillis Wheatley's work was an important part of America's story?

Applying What You've Learned

Phillis Wheatley wrote her poems about the events taking place around her. Write a short poem telling of a news event in your school or town.

Maria Mitchell
Astronomer

Maria Mitchell was born in 1818 on Nantucket Island. Lying just 30 miles off the Massachusetts coast, Nantucket was the greatest whaling port in the world.

Whaling was a dangerous business. The men were often away for years at a time, in search of the great whales which could be harvested for lamp oil. They braved fierce storms. They drifted for weeks without a hint of wind to fill the sails. They saw strange lands and new peoples. Many did not return. Those that did sailed home with only the stars to guide them.

Maria Mitchell

From the roof of her childhood home, Maria could see many of these ships at sea. Like most people of Nantucket, she came to know the skies. She watched them and learned many things. The clouds told of storms brewing. The stars formed a map to guide the ships on their voyages around the world.

In this world of water and sky, Maria Mitchell learned to love the stars. She once said of her home, "The landscape is flat and somewhat boring. The field of the heavens has greater attractions."

She also had a good teacher in her father, William Mitchell. He worked first as a schoolteacher and later as a banker. But he spent his spare time in his home observatory. He found his young daughter to be an apt pupil.

Every night the two of them would go to their rooftop. There they would plot the course of the stars. Maria took this work seriously. She kept her observations in a notebook marked "Astronomy." It was filled with many carefully written figures and charts.

No weather was bad enough to keep Maria from her work. One night it was so cold that her hands nearly froze as she recorded her measurements. The next morning she learned that two elderly neighbors had frozen to death in their little house down the street.

William Mitchell used his measurements of distances between the stars to check the accuracy of chronometers (ships' clocks) for whaling captains. One night a captain came to the Mitchells' house. He wanted his chronometer checked. Maria's mother told the man that her husband was out of town. The captain was upset. No one else on the island could fix the chronometer. And he was about to sail.

Maria Mitchell spoke up. She told the captain that she had helped her father fix many chronometers. The captain was not so sure about having a 12-year-old do such exacting work. But he had no choice. He left the instrument with Maria.

The girl used her father's sextant to measure the height of certain stars. She compared this measurement with the time on the chronometer. Slowly and carefully, she checked her results against the position of other stars. When the captain arrived the next morning, he was amazed. Maria had done a perfect job.

Maria loved her work. Her parents gave her a small closet at the foot of the stairs for a study. There she spent hours studying math books. She loved to work out problems over and over. She questioned everything she read. In her diary she wrote, "Astronomy is not stargazing. The entrance to astronomy is through mathematics."

But Maria had many other responsibilities to fill her days. As the third of 10 children, she had seven young ones to help care for. She cooked and cleaned. It seemed there were always more dishes to wash!

She also went to school beginning at age four. School was not a happy time for her. The teaching method of the day included learning long lessons by rote. The children copied the drab, moralistic lessons over and over. They had to memorize the lines. It did not matter if they could understand them. Here is an example from *The American Spelling Book.*

"O may I not go in the way of sin.
Let me not go in the way of ill men."

Stern stuff for a four-year-old!

Maria's family was Quaker. People of this religion believed in hard work and no play. They did not allow music, games, or parties.

Luckily for Maria, she had other sources of education. Her mother, a former librarian, had filled their house with books. Maria read everything in the house.

Her father taught her the wonders of nature. Young Maria collected shells and plants on her walks along the sea. She found fossils on the sandy cliffs. She and her father made the most of the opportunities for learning at hand.

Maria later wrote in her diary, "Our want of opportunity was our opportunity . . . . We are what we are partly because we had little and wanted much."

When Maria was a teenager, the Reverend Cyrus Pierce was her teacher. He demanded of his pupils that "everything be wholly, precisely right." Maria's Quaker roots had already taught her discipline. Now she sharpened her ability to observe and calculate. She later stated, "I was born of only ordinary capacity, but of extraordinary persistence."

At the age of 17, Maria opened her own school. She placed an ad in the paper for students. It was a most unusual school that opened in 1835!

In those days, often only white males went to school. But the Quakers believed in equal education for all. So, a variety of children came to the school. Rich and poor. Black and white. Girls and boys. All were welcome at the new school.

Maria's teaching methods were unusual as well. Sometimes, she began the school day before dawn. She wanted her pupils to observe the behavior of birds in the early morning. Other days began late so the pupils could observe the stars. Maria taught her students: "Learn to observe. The eye learns to see. Open yours wide to nature's [wonders]. Watch after sunset. Watch before dawn."

But Maria longed to continue her own studies. The next year she closed her school. She took a job as a librarian. The library did not open until the afternoon. So, she had all morning to study and read.

One evening in 1847 Maria was observing the stars, as was her habit. That night she made her biggest discovery. There was a new comet in the sky! She was the first person to see it! The comet was named the Maria Mitchell Comet. Maria became famous.

Maria was the first woman asked to join the American Academy of Arts and Sciences. She was also the first woman member of the American Association for the Advancement of Science. Few women were scientists in that day!

When Maria grew up, she became the first professor of astronomy at Vassar College. There she taught many students to observe and question as she had.

Maria also became a champion for women's rights. In 1873 she founded the Association for the Advancement of Women. Maria believed in equal pay and equal rights for women. All her life she had been told that women could not be scientists. She had proved this idea wrong.

Maria taught for 23 years at Vassar. She died in 1889 at the age of 71. She had proven to the world that women could equal men in the study of science. As a girl of 12, Maria Mitchell began a lifelong devotion to science that would inspire generations of women to reach for the stars.

Remembering the Facts

1. What were whales harvested for?

2. Why was knowledge of the stars important to the people of Nantucket?

3. What is a chronometer?

4. What did Maria measure with the sextant?

5. Why did Maria dislike the teaching method of Quaker schools?

6. How did Maria's parents add to her education?

7. Name two things that were unusual about Maria's school.

   (a)

   (b)

8. What did Maria discover in 1847?

9. At what college did Maria teach astronomy?

10. How did Maria work for women's rights?

Understanding the Story

11. How do you think Maria developed the skills that served her well as a scientist?

12. Maria stated, "I was born of only ordinary capacity, but of extraordinary persistence." Why do you think this quality is important for success in any field?

Getting the Main Idea

How do you think Maria Mitchell's achievements as a young girl opened the door for more women to study science?

Applying What You've Learned

Maria once wrote of her childhood, "Our want of opportunity was our opportunity. . . .We are what we are partly because we had little and wanted much." How did her Quaker childhood help her to concentrate on her goals?

Allen Jay
Underground Railroad "Conductor"

Before 1860, there were about 4 million slaves in America. Most of them lived and worked on plantations in the South. They worked hard all their lives. Their living conditions were usually very poor. Most slaves hoped that one day they might escape to freedom.

One of these slaves was Francis Henderson. He worked on a plantation from the time he was 10 years old. Francis lived with his aunt in a leaky shack that let in the wind and rain. His bed was a board propped up on a pillow. He had no blankets. Only a thin jacket kept him warm. Young Francis knew that other slaves

Allen Jay

sometimes escaped. But he had no idea how they did it. "Men would disappear all at once. A man who was working by me yesterday would be gone today. How? I knew not. I really believed that they had some great flying machine to take them through the air."

Between 1830 and 1860, many slaves did escape. But they didn't fly away as Francis imagined. They traveled to freedom on the Underground Railroad! (In 1841, when Francis was 19, he too discovered the secret of the Underground Railroad and escaped to freedom.)

The Underground Railroad was not a railroad at all. Rather, it was a secret way slaves used to get to the North. The Railroad was a network of people who helped slaves escape. Slaves stayed in houses called "stations" along the route. "Conductors" led the slaves from one station to another. "Stationmasters" fed and housed the slaves along the way.

Slaves traveled along the route in many ways. They rode hidden in wagons or boats. They rode on horseback. But usually they walked. They often traveled at night, using the North Star to guide them. During the day, they hid in swamps and forests.

Escape was dangerous. Wild animals and snakes lived in the swamps and forests. The slaves were hungry and cold. But a much greater danger awaited if they were caught. Slaves were valuable. Their owners tried to track them down, often using dogs to follow the scent. They hired slave hunters to look for runaway slaves. A slave who was caught would be severely punished.

After slavery was made illegal in the northern states (by 1800), slaves could flee to these states. But in 1850, the Fugitive Slave Law made it unsafe even there. This law stated that slave hunters could come into the northern states to capture and return a slave to the South. So, many slaves began an even longer trip to the distant land of Canada. Once in Canada, a slave was legally free.

Many people put themselves at risk to help slaves like Francis Henderson escape. They did so because they believed that slavery was wrong. These people were men, women, and children, both black and white.

Many Quakers worked on the Underground Railroad. Their religion taught them that all people were equal. Therefore, no one should be a slave. One person who helped many slaves escape was a young Quaker boy named Allen Jay. This is his story.

Allen Jay was born on October 11, 1831, in Mill Creek Meeting, Ohio. He was the oldest of five children. His parents were faithful Quakers. The children worked on the family farm in the summer. They attended school in the winter.

Allen's mother was in poor health. So it fell to him to do the family wash each Monday morning. This was not a simple process. The clothes had to be scrubbed and boiled. Bluing and starch had to be applied. (Bluing kept white clothes white.) Then the clothes had to be hung out to dry. It was a big job for a small boy. But after he was done, Allen had the rest of the day off to fish, hunt, or swim.

Each Sunday, the Jay family went to meeting (Quaker religious services). Often in meeting, someone would speak about the Underground Railroad. Many of the Quakers were in favor of this work; some were not. The Jay home was a "station" on the Railroad.

One day, Allen was outside doing the wash. The family doctor, who was an abolitionist (a person against slavery), rode up. He told Mr. Jay, Allen's father, that there was a runaway slave hiding in the woods nearby. The slave was being chased by his master and others. Allen heard and understood all of this although he was only 11.

Mr. Jay turned to Allen and said, "I am going out back of the house to work. If a black man comes to the gate, take him down in the cornfield and hide him under that big walnut tree. But don't tell me or anyone else."

Soon the man came. His feet were bleeding and his clothes torn. Allen said he could hide in the cornfield. At first, the man was afraid. But when Allen gave his name, the man knew he was safe.

Allen took the man to the walnut tree and told him to stay there. Allen returned to his home. There, his mother was fixing a basket of food and a pitcher of milk. Soon she said, "Allen, if you know anyone who is hungry, you might take this basket to him."

Allen started off with the food. The escaped slave heard him coming and was afraid. So he pulled out a gun and pointed it at Allen. When he saw who it was, he smiled. Allen gave him the food and said he would be back after dark.

About that time, a group of men rode up to the farm on horseback. They asked Mr. Jay if he had seen a black man going by. Mr. Jay was able to say truthfully that he had not. (Quakers were taught never to lie.) Allen kept out of sight. The men roughly pushed Mr. Jay aside and threatened to search the house. Mr. Jay told them they were welcome to look around, but only if they had a search warrant. The men argued with and threatened Mr. Jay, but finally they rode off, promising to return.

When it was growing dark, Mr. Jay began to hitch up the horse, Old Jack, to the buggy. He then came to the house and asked Allen how he would like to go to his grandfather's house. Allen knew at once what his father meant. Mr. Jay added, "If you know anybody you think ought to go, take him along."

Allen and the escaped slave began the journey. The man could see that Allen was a little nervous. So to show he meant no harm, he offered to let Allen hold the pistol. But, he added, "If anyone comes to take me, you must stop and let me out and give me the pistol. For I am never going to be taken back."

Four hours later, Allen and the escaped slave reached Allen's grandfather's farm. Allen's grandfather called Allen's uncle, Levi Jay. Soon, Levi and the slave were riding north to the next "station." The Jays learned later that the escaped slave had reached the safety of Canada. This was the first time, but not the last, that young Allen Jay was a "conductor" on the Underground Railroad.

Allen Jay grew up to become a traveling Quaker preacher. He visited groups of Quakers in America and in Europe. He was much in demand as a public speaker. This is amazing, because Allen was born with a hole in the roof of his mouth. His speech was difficult to understand at times. Yet, his message of peace and love was so strong that people flocked to hear him.

Allen Jay also worked as a teacher. He became a national leader in Quaker education. For years, he worked to get more funds for Quaker colleges. He was extremely successful at this job.

When Allen Jay was 80 years old, he wrote down the story of his part in the Underground Railroad in his autobiography, *The Autobiography of Allen Jay.* He died on May 8, 1910, one of the most beloved and famous of all Quakers.

The Underground Railroad kept running until after the Civil War. When the South was defeated in 1865, slavery was brought to an end. By then, more than 60,000 runaway slaves had already taken the Underground Railroad to freedom. Long after the Underground Railroad was no longer needed, its stories lived on—including the story of a young boy who took on the brave and dangerous work of a man.

Remembering the Facts

1. What was the Underground Railroad?

2. What was the job of a "conductor" on the Underground Railroad?

3. What was the greatest danger faced by a slave who was trying to escape?

4. What was the Fugitive Slave Law?

5. Why did many Quakers work on the Underground Railroad?

6. Why did Mr. Jay ask Allen to help the escaped slave instead of doing so himself?

7. What happened to the escaped slave Allen Jay helped?

8. Name two kinds of work Allen Jay did as an adult.

   (a)

   (b)

9. Why did the Underground Railroad come to an end?

10. About how many slaves traveled to freedom on the Underground Railroad?

Understanding the Story

11. Many slaves wanted to escape to the North. But the way to get on the Underground Railroad was a closely guarded secret. Why do you think this was so?

12. Why do you think many people, both black and white, Northerners and Southerners, were willing to risk their lives to help slaves escape?

Getting the Main Idea

The trip north to Canada was long and dangerous. Many who tried did not make it. Why do you think some slaves made up their minds to try it? Why do you think others chose to stay where they were?

Applying What You've Learned

Imagine you are a slave escaping to freedom. Write a paragraph telling about your most frightening moment along the way.

Mary Jane Dilworth
Teacher

The story of the Utah Territory begins in the state of New York. It was in New York, in 1830, that Joseph Smith founded a new church called The Church of Jesus Christ of Latter-Day Saints. Members of the church were called Latter-Day Saints (LDS) or Mormons.

Mary Jane Dilworth

The Mormons had beliefs that were very different from those of other Christian churches. They believed their church to be the true church of Jesus restored to Earth after years of spiritual darkness. In addition to the Bible, they had three other holy books. They also believed that men could have more than one wife at a time (polygamy).

Many other Christian groups were threatened by these nontraditional beliefs. The Mormons were pushed west to Illinois. There, they founded the town of Nauvoo. By the early 1840's, Nauvoo was the largest city in Illinois.

But non-Mormons in Illinois hated the Mormons, too. They burned Mormon farms and crops. They burned much of the town of Nauvoo. On June 27, 1844, a mob murdered Joseph Smith and his brother Hyrum.

A new leader took over. Brigham Young was determined to follow the dream of Joseph Smith. He wanted to establish a new home for the Mormons in the desert lands of the far West. He called upon all Mormons to come to Nauvoo. From there they would begin the long, dangerous journey west.

One of the many families who made the journey was the Dilworth family. They were Quakers living in Pennsylvania when they heard of the new religion. Soon they decided to join the new church. Like many other Mormons, they were forced from their home by those who feared and misunderstood them. The Dilworths had eight children—seven girls and one boy. Mary Jane Dilworth, born in 1832, was one of the younger children. She was later to play an important role in the settling of Utah. She would become Utah's first teacher.

Mary Jane was 14 when her family arrived in Nauvoo. Her family had hoped to settle there. They had not yet heard the news of the burning of the town. What a shock awaited them as they stepped ashore from the riverboat as it docked at Nauvoo! The pretty little town was a shell of its former self.

The Dilworth family did not remain long in Nauvoo. It was important that they get started on the trip west before the weather got cold.

In April 1846, thousands of Mormons set out. For the first few weeks, the trip was exciting. The weather was fine, and the children ran alongside the wagons. It all seemed like a great adventure.

Then came the rains. Day after day, the children huddled inside the wagons. They quickly became bored. Mary Jane Dilworth took charge. Reaching into her bag, she brought out a small blue speller. She convinced the children to play school. Every day, she taught them from her speller. If they listened well, she rewarded them with a story. Mary Jane kept up the lessons until the group reached Council Bluffs, Iowa.

Council Bluffs was the site the Mormons had chosen to camp for the winter. "School" was over for the older children who had chores to do in camp. The boys took care of the cattle, cut hay, and chopped wood. The girls washed, ironed, cooked, and took care of the babies.

Since Mary Jane was good with children, she got the job of taking care of a dozen young children. She made up rhymes and songs to teach them their ABC's. She told them stories. She taught them songs and games.

She began teaching the children to read. One day, as she was giving lessons, Brigham Young came by to watch. He was so impressed, he sent his son for lessons with Mary Jane's group.

It was a terrible winter for the Mormons. Their shelters had been quickly built and did not keep out the cold and rain. Hundreds of people got sick. Many died.

It got so cold, the children were forced to stay inside. They became restless from being cooped up. Fifteen-year-old Mary Jane decided to begin school for the older children again. Day after day she kept them at their lessons and away from thoughts about their surroundings.

Finally, on June 17, 1847, the Mormons left their winter quarters. Once again, they were on the way to find their new home. The miles of prairie seemed endless. For three months of burning summer, the group moved west. Mary Jane kept her small charges happy and busy.

In July, Brigham Young left the main body of travelers behind. He led an advance party of about 170 Mormons into the Great Salt Lake valley. They arrived on July 24, 1846. "This is the place," he said as he looked down over the wide valley.

By early September, the rest of the Mormons were climbing the slope toward the top of the Continental Divide. One night, they camped on the Sweetwater River in Wyoming. Suddenly, excitement ran through the camp. Brigham Young had returned from the Salt Lake valley. He began to speak to the group.

Mary Jane stood on the edge of the crowd. Many children stood close to her. When Brigham Young finished speaking, he walked over to Mary Jane.

"Sister Dilworth," he began, "I have a special mission for you. As soon as we reach our new home, I want you to start a school for the younger children. Any children who wish to may attend, and I encourage all to do so. God bless you."

A mission was a high calling for a Mormon. Mary Jane knew she would do everything in her power to build a wonderful school in the new land.

In October, Mary Jane's group finally emerged from the canyons east of the Salt Lake valley. They stopped and stared at the valley before them. It was full of tall grasses and shrubs. In the distance lay the Great Salt Lake. Ringing the huge valley were tall blue mountains. It looked like a safe home at last for the Mormons.

Already a new city was springing up. Streets were laid out. They were broad and straight. A few cabins had already been built. But the newcomers would live in the fort until they could build their own cabins. The fort was an enclosed area surrounded by cabins. In the center of the fort was a large open square area.

Sixteen-year-old Mary Jane Dilworth wasted no time in readying a site for her new school. She got some men to set up an army tent in one corner of the square. She had others make benches from logs that were too short to use for building cabins. Her desk was a seat which had been taken out of a wagon.

Mary Jane went through town collecting books for the school. She found very few. But she did collect one speller, two readers, and one arithmetic book.

On October 19, just two weeks after she arrived in the Salt Lake valley, Mary Jane opened her school. It was the first school in what would later become the state of Utah.

The main subjects taught in the new school were reading, writing, and arithmetic. Mary Jane also had her students read and memorize Bible verses. The students learned their times tables and had spelling bees. Mary Jane believed in using many drills to go over and over the material being taught. She knew that what the children learned well, they would not forget.

On November 11, 1848, at the age of 17, Mary Jane married Francis Hammond. Three years later, her husband was sent as a missionary of The Church of Jesus Christ of Latter-Day Saints to the Hawaiian Islands. Mary Jane and the couple's baby went with him. They hoped to teach others there about their faith.

The young couple stayed in Hawaii for six years. Mary Jane continued her teaching career, working at a school for young islanders. She also cooked and sewed for the unmarried Mormon missionaries serving in Hawaii.

Later, Mary Jane and her husband settled in Huntsville, Utah. There, Mary Jane again taught school. She died in Huntsville on June 6, 1877, at the age of 45.

Mary Jane's grave was the first in the Huntsville cemetery. Its marker reads as follows:

IN HONOR
OF
The First School Teacher of Utah
Mrs. Mary Jane Dilworth Hammond

A school in Salt Lake City has been named after Mary Jane. It is called the Mary Jane Dilworth Elementary School. What a beautiful tribute to the young girl who loved teaching!

Remembering the Facts

1. Why weren't the Mormons popular with their neighbors?

2. What town did the Mormons found in Illinois?

3. Who led the Mormons from Nauvoo to Utah?

4. How did Mary Jane Dilworth begin teaching the children on the wagon train?

5. Where did the Mormons camp for the winter?

6. What mission did Brigham Young give Mary Jane?

7. Where did Mary Jane set up her first school?

8. Why did Mary Jane use many drills in her teaching?

9. Where did Mary Jane and her husband serve as missionaries?

10. What building in Salt Lake City is named after Mary Jane?

Understanding the Story

11. How do you think the subjects taught in Mary Jane's school would be the same and different from those taught in an elementary school today?

12. What qualities do you think are most important for a successful teacher? In what ways do you think Mary Jane Dilworth exhibited these qualities?

Getting the Main Idea

One of the mottos of The Church of Jesus Christ of Latter-Day Saints is "The glory of God is intelligence." How do you think Mary Jane Dilworth was true to this teaching?

Applying What You've Learned

Imagine that you've been asked to start a school for young children. You have four textbooks: a speller, two readers, and one arithmetic book. How would you schedule the day using only these materials (no paper or pencils) and your own imagination?

Orion Howe
Civil War Drummer Boy

To join the U.S. Army today, you must show a birth certificate to prove you are 18 or older. In the days of the Civil War (1861–1865) soldiers were also supposed to be over 18. But often they were far younger.

Both the Union (Northern) and Confederate (Southern) armies were desperate for soldiers. If a boy looked big enough to carry a musket, he was accepted without question. Those who were small had to show proof of their age. Or they simply could swear that they were 18.

Orion Howe

Many boys were so eager to join the fight that they lied about their ages. Over 800,000 Union soldiers were under 17. Two-hundred thousands were 16. And 100,000 Union soldiers were only 15 years old. The same held true for the Confederates.

Boys between 10 and 16 served on the battlefield in other ways. Some of these boys joined the Navy as "powder monkeys." Their job was to carry gunpowder aboard the ships. Other boys joined the army to play the drums or the fife (a small instrument similar to a flute). Each company in the army could have two musicians. That made about 20 musicians in a regiment. Over 40,000 boy musicians served in the Civil War.

At that time, there were no telephones or walkie-talkies to link officers and their men on the battlefield. Through the drummers, officers gave orders to their troops. Different rhythm patterns meant different actions on the field.

Drummer boys and fifers (fife players) also inspired the troops. They played beats for the soldiers to march to. They played favorite battle songs. Their music helped keep up the morale of the weary soldiers.

One of the most famous of these Civil War drummer boys was Orion Howe. He was only 13 when he served in the Union Army. His brother, Lyston Howe, was only 10.

The boys' father, William Howe, was a carpenter. He had been a fifer in the Mexican War. When his two sons, Orion and Lyston, were very young, he gave them each a drum. He taught the boys how to play. The two boys learned the rhythms quickly.

Their grandmother made each of them a uniform of white pants and a blue jacket. The two boys played at church picnics, birthday parties, and political rallies. Everyone loved them (except maybe their neighbors, who grew tired of the noise).

When the Civil War broke out in April of 1861, William Howe enlisted in a Union regiment as a fifer. He took Lyston, who was 10, along with him to serve as a drummer.

Orion, a promising student, was left behind to continue his studies. He was surely not pleased to be at a desk, while his little brother was off at war! But he did as he was told.

By November, most of the older boys in the school had enlisted. Some boys had already seen action in the war and had returned to school missing arms or legs. The only teachers left were old men or preachers. Orion was determined not to be left out of the great adventure. So, he joined up with the 55th Illinois Regiment in which his father was the fife major. William Howe led 10 fifers and 10 drummers (including his two sons).

The 55th Illinois marched south to Memphis, Tennessee. There it made camp. At first, army life was exciting. The boys loved camping outdoors, freed from school and chores at home.

In camp, the days went by a plan. Orion had to get up early to play reveille (the wake-up call). When breakfast was ready, another series of drumbeats gave everyone the message.

Next, sick call was tapped out. Those who were sick went to the hospital tent. The rest of the men did chores. Some cut wood. Others cleaned up. There was always plenty to do.

At 8:00 A.M., the fourth drum call of the day went out. That was the signal for the changing of the guard. Those who had been on guard all night were replaced with other men. After that, the colonel made his morning inspection of the camp.

After inspection, the drum call announced that it was time for morning drills. Some of the time, the troops drilled all morning. Other times they drilled for only an hour. Then they had free time until the sixth drum roll called everyone to the noon meal.

After this meal, the entire regiment assembled for dress parade. The soldiers stood at attention, grouped by companies. The musicians played battle songs. Then the colonel gave the orders of the day. There might be more drills or a speech. Then there was free time until it was time to call the men to dinner. Another drum roll signaled that it was time for evening roll call. Finally, the drummers ended the day by playing taps.

Orion liked military life. The men treated him well. It was exciting being a part of the camp. And the campsite at Memphis was pleasant. But things were about to change.

In November 1862, the regiment marched to a spot not far from Vicksburg, Mississippi. For months they camped in a swampy spot across the Mississippi River from Vicksburg. The soldiers put up with snakes, rats, and bugs. When the river flooded, they were nearly washed downstream. William Howe got sick and was sent home. That left his two boys on their own in the army.

Vicksburg sat high on a bluff overlooking the river. It had been well armed by the Confederate Army. It would be a hard site to capture. But both sides knew that Vicksburg was the key to the war. The Union Army had almost completely encircled the Confederacy and controlled all of the Mississippi except for the 200 miles south of Vicksburg. Farmers in the North needed the river to ship their crops down to New Orleans and then off to Europe. The heavy guns of Vicksburg were blocking the way. It became clear that Vicksburg had to be taken at all costs. A Union victory at Vicksburg would mean that the entire river would be open again.

The Union Army tried several attacks, facing the enemy head-on. It became clear this would never work. The Union generals' new plan was to circle around and attack Vicksburg from the rear. The 55th Illinois began marching south. They reached Hard Times, Louisiana, on May 11, 1863. Steamboats ferried the men across the river to the Mississippi side. Then they began marching north.

They passed through the little town of Raymond, Mississippi, 30 miles from Vicksburg. The whole town had been turned into a huge hospital ward. Everywhere there were injured and dying men from other Union regiments. Row after row of graves bordered the road. Worst of all were the stacks of legs and arms which had been cut off the wounded soldiers. Orion began to realize the true horrors of war.

A few days later, the attack on Vicksburg began again. The Confederates had dug in on the high ground. As the Union soldiers attacked, the Confederate soldiers easily cut them down. Soon, the Union regiments on both sides of the 55th Illinois had retreated. The 55th Illinois was trapped on three sides. Many men were being killed or wounded.

Since Orion Howe and the other drummers did not carry guns, they were supposed to stay in the rear, away from the fighting. But Orion went forward with the troops. He thought it was his duty to try and help those who were wounded. Most of the men were dead or beyond help. Orion patched the wounds that did not seem too serious. Then he helped the men crawl out of the line of fire.

The sergeant ordered Orion to the rear. He told him the best way he could help would be to get more ammunition for the soldiers who were almost out. Orion got the idea of collecting cartridges from the dead and wounded. He ran across the battle-field gathering cartridge boxes.

But his work was not enough. Someone had to get through to the supply wagons in the rear and ask for more ammunition. Orion and three other drummers volunteered for the job. The colonel told them to ask for 500 rounds of 54-caliber ammunition.

The boys raced down the road. Confederate sharpshooters took aim and began firing at them. Three of the boys were hit and killed. Orion was hit in the thigh. But he knew he had to get through. On he stumbled, until he found the supplies. His leg was covered with blood, but he would not stop until he had delivered his message. "Send cartridges," he yelled. "Caliber 54." Then he fainted from the pain.

Orion Howe's wound was not serious, but it kept him in the hospital for weeks. The attacks on Vicksburg continued for 47 days. In the end, Vicksburg surrendered to the Union Army on July 4, 1863.

The "boy hero of Vicksburg" returned to the army when he was well. On Christmas Day, 1863, he was promoted to the rank of corporal. He worked as an orderly for General Morgan L. Smith. One day, while he was delivering a message for the general, he was shot in the arm and the chest. Luckily, he recovered from these wounds.

After the war, Orion won an appointment to the U.S. Naval Academy. He had letters of recommendation from General William T. Sherman and President Abraham Lincoln. After two years in the Academy, he tired of its strict rules. He left and joined the merchant marine. His ship was wrecked and he nearly drowned in 1867.

Orion left the service and headed for the "wild west." He became a scout for the army and was nearly killed in a battle with Indians in 1873.

After a boyhood of high adventure and close calls, Orion went to New York where he studied to become a dentist. He settled in Nebraska and worked as a dentist for many years.

On April 23, 1897, Orion P. Howe received a package in the mail. His boyhood bravery had been rewarded with the highest military award: the Medal of Honor. Orion Howe went on to live a long, full life. He died on January 27, 1930, at the age of 82.

Remembering the Facts

1. Why was it easy for boys under 18 to join the army during the Civil War?

2. Name two ways boys ages 10 to 16 served in the army, other than as soldiers.

   (a)   (b)

3. What were the two main jobs of the drummers?

   (a)

   (b)

4. Why was Orion Howe unhappy about being in school in 1861?

5. Which regiment did Orion and his brother Lyston join?

6. Why was Vicksburg an important city for both sides to win?

7. Why did the Union generals decide to circle around and attack Vicksburg from the rear?

8. Why didn't Orion stay in the rear with the other drummers?

9. In what two ways did Orion get more ammunition for the troops?

   (a)

   (b)

10. What military award did Orion receive in 1897?

Understanding the Story

11. Why do you think so many young boys were eager to join the fighting during the Civil War?

12. Why do you think Orion was unable to complete his education at the U.S. Naval Academy?

Getting the Main Idea

Why do you think Orion Howe became known as the "boy hero of Vicksburg"? In what ways do you think his actions were heroic and inspired the troops?

Applying What You've Learned

Imagine that you are a drummer in either the Union or Confederate Army. Write a paragraph telling about a day in your life.

Shirley Temple
Actress

The Great Depression was the worst economic crisis in American history. It began with the stock market crash on October 29, 1929. It lasted through the 1930's. During this time, millions of people were out of work.

Banks closed, taking with them the life savings of many workers. Businesses failed. People lost their homes and farms. Bread lines formed. Soup kitchens gave out food. Men stood on street corners selling apples for a nickel. It was a time of deep national despair. The song that expressed the feeling of the times was, "Brother, Can You Spare a Dime?"

Shirley Temple

Into these hard times a light came. That light was a little girl named Shirley Temple. President Franklin D. Roosevelt said of her: "The spirit of the people is lower than at any other time during this depression. It is a splendid thing that for just 15 cents an American can go to a movie and look at the smiling face of a baby and forget his troubles."

Shirley Temple was born on April 23, 1928. Her mother said she was born an actress. When she was eight months old, Shirley tried to dance in her crib. When she began to walk at 12 months, she walked on her toes. It was as if she was dancing.

When Shirley was three, she started dancing lessons. Her mother signed her up at Meglin Dance Studio. It was a school that taught children gymnastics, dance, acting, and singing. From the start, Shirley learned very quickly.

In 1932, Shirley was spotted by a movie director. He was filming a series of short films called *Baby Burlesks.* These films were spoofs on current hit movies. In these short films, small children were dressed in diapers. They were given other props to look like the characters they were playing.

Shirley's first role was in a nine-minute film called *War Babies.* It was a takeoff on the hit movie *What Price Glory?* Shirley played a French girl. She wore a lace blouse, a garter below her knee, a rose in her hair, and a diaper. Other tots played baby soldiers.

The *Baby Burlesks* series was wildly popular. Shirley starred in eight of the films that year. She was earning $10 a day, $40 for a four-day workweek. That was a lot of money during the Depression. Her father was in danger of losing his job by then, so the money she earned was no small thing.

Making movies was hard work. In her autobiography, Shirley Temple described her life as a four-year-old star:

> "It is not easy to be a Hollywood starlet. Often starlets are knocked to the floor. Or pricked by their diaper pins. The hours are long. Your hair and teeth must always be clean. The same goes for your white socks. . . . Starlets must be cheerful. . . . Starlets must always be prepared. . . . Being a starlet is a hard life, especially when you are four years old."

The studio also had strict rules. Children who did not obey had to spend "time out" in a large black soundproof box. Inside, it was hot. There was no source of fresh air. A large block of ice in one corner chilled the stale air. It also made a puddle on the floor. A child placed in "the box" had no dry place to sit. For a child who had been acting under hot lights, the cold box often meant getting sick later.

The studios at this time did not care about people's rights. They were only concerned about getting the movie done on time. Children worked even if they were sick or injured. Today's child labor laws would have prevented many of these abuses.

Shirley quickly learned how to cope. As she says, "Pay attention. Be alert. Do as I was told, when and how. Get it right the first time. No mistakes, and no wasted time."

Shirley did better than most children in this regard. She had a quick memory. She could hear her lines once and remember them. Seeing a dance step, she could repeat it perfectly. She was so good that directors could usually film her scenes in only one "take." Soon Shirley had the nickname "One-Take Temple."

The next year, the studio went bankrupt. Shirley was five years old and out of work! One afternoon, she and her mother went to the Fox Wilshire Theater to see a movie. While they were there, they met a man who changed their lives.

The man was Jay Gorney, a songwriter. He was working on the movie *Stand Up and Cheer.* The studio was looking for a child to act in the movie. Jay Gorney saw Shirley in the lobby of the theater that day. He said to his wife, "Have you ever seen a cuter child?" Quickly, he went up to Shirley's mother. He asked her if Shirley would be interested in a role in a major motion picture.

Shirley was a hit—a big one. The studio offered her a seven-year contract. She starred in six more movies that year. The best known of these is *Little Miss Marker.* She was also famous for singing the song "On the Good Ship Lollipop."

The critics loved Shirley. Some of their comments were:

"The child is absolutely irresistible."

"The women all gush over her."

"No more engaging child has ever been seen on the screen."

By the time Shirley was seven years old, she was the biggest box office draw in America. Shirley's films showed her as a brave, spunky girl. She warmed the hearts of Americans who had been battered by the Depression.

In 1935, Shirley won an Oscar—the highest award given to a motion picture actor or actress. It was the first miniature Academy Award ever given to a child. It read: "Shirley Temple (has) brought more happiness to millions of children and grownups than any other child of her years in the history of the world."

She was asked to put her hand and footprints into cement at the famous Grauman's Chinese Theater. Next to the prints, she wrote "Love to you all." At seven, she was a Hollywood immortal.

The money began rolling in. By the time she was 10, she was making more money than the president of General Motors. Shirley's father invested her money for her. She would get it when she was 21. Until then she got an allowance of five dollars a week.

Shirley Temple products began to appear everywhere. Companies made Shirley Temple dresses, jewelry, china, soap, toys, coats, hats, shoes, books, hair ribbons, purses, underwear, and mugs. Most popular of all were the Shirley Temple dolls. Shirley was "America's Sweetheart" and she could sell anything. By the time Shirley was 12, her fortune was between 3 and 5 million dollars.

By age 10, Shirley had starred in 17 major pictures. Each was a huge success. All this fame had its price. She was leading a childhood that could not be normal, no matter how hard her parents tried. When she went out, she was driven in a bulletproof car. She went home to a house surrounded by a high wall. There were alarms, armed guards, and barred windows.

Shirley lived isolated from other children. She didn't go to school; she was tutored. She had a few playmates. But they always had to play at her house.

Shirley accepted her role as America's princess. She never complained. As an adult looking back on her childhood, she still insisted she wouldn't change a thing.

When Shirley began to grow up, her popularity started to fade. People weren't interested in seeing a teenage Shirley. By 1939, she began a rapid slide down the list of box-office stars. The magic years had come to an end.

Shirley did not retire right away. For a few years she worked on radio shows, made movies, and hosted television shows. And she entered seventh grade at a private girls' school. For the first time, she had a nearly normal social life.

As an adult, Shirley Temple entered politics. In 1967, she ran for the U.S. House of Representatives. In 1969, she was appointed U.S. delegate to the United Nations.

President Ford appointed Shirley as Ambassador to Ghana. Then, in 1976, he brought her to the White House as Chief of Protocol. She was the first woman to fill that post.

In 1990, President Bush appointed Shirley as Ambassador to Czechoslovakia. This was her most challenging job of all.

Shirley Temple is married to Charles Black. She now goes by the name Shirley Temple Black. She has three children.

As a child, Shirley Temple cheered an entire nation that was deep in despair. Though her star faded when she was no longer wanted on movie sets, she found a way to shine again—on a very different kind of stage. As an important person on the stage of world politics, the former child star was serving her country once again.

Remembering the Facts

1. What was the Great Depression?

2. How old was Shirley when the stock market crashed?

3. In what short film series did Shirley star at age three?

4. What was "the box" used for in the studio?

5. Why did Shirley get the nickname "One-Take Temple"?

6. What was Shirley's first full-length movie?

7. What award did Shirley get in 1935?

8. In what ways was Shirley denied a normal childhood?

9. Why did her days as a star end when she reached her teens?

10. In what field has Shirley worked as an adult?

Understanding the Story

11. Why do you think it was Shirley (rather than another movie star) who was able to cheer up America during the Depression?

12. Shirley's childhood was far from "normal." Do you think any child star can live a "normal" lifestyle? Why or why not?

Getting the Main Idea

What role do you think the arts play in helping us live fuller, richer lives?

Applying What You've Learned

When Shirley became a star, companies started making Shirley Temple "products." What modern parallels can you find for this? Write a paragraph telling about one or more modern examples of mass marketing of a star.

Melba Pattillo
Civil Rights Activist

As an American citizen, you have certain rights. If you're hungry, you can go into a restaurant and order food. If you're thirsty, you can drink from any water fountain. You can use public rest rooms. You can travel on the bus or train and sit wherever you want.

But a black citizen living in the South before 1960 couldn't do any of these things. In the southern states, black people and white people were segregated (kept separate) in nearly all aspects of life.

Separate water fountains and rest rooms had signs reading "White" or "Colored." Some restaurants were for white people only. Others were for black people. Black people had to sit in the back of buses and trains.

Melba Pattillo

Black people who did not obey these rules could be arrested. After all, they were breaking state law. The law was unfair. But it was the way it had always been since the slaves were freed after the Civil War.

There were separate schools for black people and white people, too. The schools were not of equal quality. White schools were well-kept buildings with trained teachers and new books. Black children went to school in old buildings. Their teachers were often poorly trained. And they used the old books that the white schools were throwing away.

Things were about to change. In 1954, the United States Supreme Court ruled in a case called *Brown* v. *Board of Education of Topeka.* The Court ruled that segregated schools were not equal. It ordered that the schools be integrated (made available to people of all races).

Many white people in the South were stunned. Their segregated way of life was suddenly illegal. They could not imagine white and black children going to school together. These people fought any efforts to integrate the schools. Many southern schools were not integrated until 10 to 20 years after the Court's ruling.

In Little Rock, Arkansas, a dramatic example of integration was about to unfold. The events that took place shocked the nation. A group of nine black students was chosen to integrate Central High School. Later they became known as "The Little Rock Nine." One of these students was Melba Pattillo.

Melba was born on December 7, 1941. It was the same day the Japanese bombed Pearl Harbor, Hawaii. Melba's mother had been one of the first few African Americans to integrate the University of Arkansas.

Melba remembers being afraid of white people from the time she was three years old. By the time she was four, she was asking hard questions. "Why do white people write 'Colored' on all the ugly drinking fountains, the dirty rest rooms, and the back of the buses?" she asked. When Melba was five, a white man refused to let her ride on the merry-go-round in the park. "There was no space for me on that merry-go-round no matter how many saddles stood empty," she later said. It was a hard way to live.

Melba was lucky to come from a strong, loving family. Her mother had a master's degree and taught seventh-grade English. Her grandmother gave her spiritual strength. She taught Melba to rely on the Bible's teachings. She told Melba, "Dignity is a state of mind, just like freedom. These are both gifts from God that no one can take away unless you allow them to."

Melba was 12 years old the day the Court ruled that segregated schools were against the law. Her teacher told her seventh-grade class about the ruling. Shaking from fear, the teacher told the children to walk home in groups. No one knew what might happen. But Melba struck out on her own. On the way home, she was attacked by a white man who was furious about the ruling. He tried to rape the little girl, but a friend came to her rescue. It was clear that school integration would not come easily.

In 1957, the Little Rock school board agreed to allow nine black students to attend Central High School. The schools asked for volunteers. Melba and a number of others signed up right away.

Nine students were chosen: Melba Pattillo, Ernest Green, Carlotta Walls, Minniejean Brown, Thelma Mothershed, Elizabeth Eckford, Terrence Roberts, Gloria Ray, and Jefferson Thomas. The students knew it would be a hard fight. But each believed strongly in freedom and equality. But none of them knew that their lives would be in danger.

On the first day of school in the fall of 1957, Governor Faubus ordered the Arkansas National Guard to surround Central High School. He ordered that only white students were to be allowed inside. For the next three weeks, the nine black students stayed home.

Then a federal court judge ordered Faubus to remove the troops. The black students were brought into the school through a side door. Outside, an angry mob attacked black and white reporters nearby. Many parents kept their children home from school.

All of this was reported in detail on the evening news. The entire nation watched in horror. The Little Rock Nine watched the full story on their televisions as well.

That night, President Eisenhower sent in military troops. Troops from the 101st Airborne Division, jeeps, and helicopters arrived on the scene. The next morning, the students were picked up by soldiers. They rode in one station wagon. An armed guard rode in back and in front of the students.

For the next few months, soldiers brought the students to school. Each student was given an armed guard who followed him or her from class to class inside the school. Melba's soldier was named Danny. He told the girl, "You will have to become a soldier. Never let your enemy know what you are feeling. Never let them see you cry."

After awhile, the troops were withdrawn from the halls. (They remained outside the school.) Then things got much worse for the students. White students would tease them, attack them, or ruin their clothing. The abuse went on and on.

Finally, one of the girls had enough. A student who picked at her constantly finally made her snap. She poured a bowl of chili on his head. Black cafeteria workers cheered. But the girl was expelled. Now the white students passed around cards reading "One down. Eight to go."

But the remaining eight lasted the whole year. In May, Ernest Green (the only senior in the group) graduated with the class of 1958. He became the first black person to graduate from Central High School.

At first there were some white students who tried to be nice to the black students. But they suffered abuse from those fighting for segregation. Most of the teachers didn't want the black students in the school either, so they were of little help.

Most of the black community stood behind the Little Rock Nine. They praised their bravery. But a number of black adults thought that the Little Rock Nine was just causing trouble for themselves and the black community as a whole.

Finally, that first long year was over. In the summer of 1958, Governor Faubus tried to get a court order to stop the students from returning to school. At first he was given a three-year delay. But a higher court reversed the ruling. Schools would open. The black students would attend.

Rather than stand for the integration of his school system, Governor Faubus ordered all Little Rock high schools to be closed. The white community was furious. They vented their fury on the remaining seven black students and their families, who received many midnight phone calls and death threats.

Civil rights leaders feared for the students' lives. Finally, the students were sent out of state. They lived with other families and finished high school.

Two years later, two more black students attended Central High School. In schools across the South, more brave black students slowly broke down barriers in schools and colleges. The Little Rock Nine became a symbol of those many students.

During that difficult year at Central High School, Melba kept a diary. She recorded events that happened. She wrote about her feelings. Her mother kept notes and newspaper clippings. When Melba was 18, she began a book about her experiences. But the past was too painful for her to relive. Her book, *Warriors Don't Cry*, was not published until she was a woman of 53.

In 1987, the Little Rock Nine had a 30-year reunion. They met on the steps at Central High School. Cameras flashed. Reporters asked questions. Fans asked for autographs.

"What was it like to attend Central?" asked one reporter.

"I got up every morning, polished my saddle shoes, and went off to war," Melba replied. "It was like being a soldier on a battlefield. . . . While most teenage girls were listening to Buddy Holly's 'Peggy Sue', watching Elvis gyrate (swing his hips), and collecting crinoline (starchy, full) slips, I was escaping the hanging rope of a lynch mob, dodging lighted sticks of dynamite, and washing away burning acid sprayed into my eyes."

The Little Rock Nine was then warmly welcomed by Governor Bill Clinton (soon to be President of the United States). But an even more exciting welcome was about to happen. As the group stood on the steps, the door to the school swung open. A black teenager came out to introduce himself. "Good morning. I am Derrick Noble, president of the student body. Welcome to Central High School." The Little Rock Nine had won! Melba Pattillo, and other brave young people like her, had changed the course of history.

Remembering the Facts

1. What is segregation?

2. What was the ruling of the Supreme Court in *Brown* v. *Board of Education of Topeka?*

3. How did Melba's grandmother give her strength?

4. What did Governor Faubus do when school opened in 1957?

5. How did President Eisenhower react?

6. At what point in the school year did things suddenly get much worse for the Little Rock Nine?

7. Why didn't the black students return to Central the next year?

8. What is the title of Melba Pattillo's book?

9. Why did Melba Pattillo wait so long to publish her story?

10. How were the Little Rock Nine greeted when they returned to Little Rock 30 years later?

Understanding the Story

11. Why do you think that many members of the black community in Little Rock did not support the students?

12. The nine students chosen to integrate Central were carefully selected. What characteristics do you think the school board looked for? Why?

Getting the Main Idea

Why do you think the Little Rock Nine became a symbol of the entire struggle to integrate the schools in the South?

Applying What You've Learned

Imagine you are one of the Little Rock Nine. As a high school student, you move from class to class during the day. You eat in the cafeteria. Physical education is required of all students. You take five other classes. Write a paragraph telling which parts of your day at school are the hardest and why.

S.E. Hinton
Author

In the 1960's, books for teenagers told stories of carefree youth. Girls' books talked about boys and dating. Books for boys centered on sports or adventure. Characters were often too good to be real and far removed from the lives of most teens.

S.E. Hinton

Into this warm and fuzzy world came S.E. Hinton's book *The Outsiders* in 1967. This gritty, realistic tale changed forever the way young adult books were written. S.E. Hinton's story of real teenagers with real problems remains a classic 25 years later. It is one of the most important and widely read books in the field of literature for young adults. It was written when the author was 16 years old!

S.E. (Susan Eloise) Hinton was born in Tulsa, Oklahoma, on April 22, 1950. As a young girl she loved to read. She began writing when she was eight. Susan also liked horses. She hoped to be a cattle rancher when she grew up.

Susan was a shy child. She felt more at ease with boys than girls. She enjoyed the active games of boys more than the quieter ones most girls played.

Susan went to Will Rogers High School in Tulsa. It was a very large school. Everyone had split into groups. The rich kids were called the Socs (for socials). The poor kids were the Greasers. Susan had friends in both groups. But she thought of herself as an "outsider," not really a part of either group.

The two groups were rivals. They never mixed unless they were fighting. Sometimes the violence got out of hand. Members of both groups were injured or killed.

When Susan was in high school, her father died of cancer. During his illness, she began writing *The Outsiders*. This helped her work through her grief.

The Outsiders is based on things that happened during Susan's high school years. It deals with the rivalry between two gangs, the Socs and the Greasers. In the story, the fighting between the two gangs leads to the death of members of both gangs.

The story is told by 14-year-old Ponyboy Curtis. Ponyboy is a Greaser. An orphan, he lives with his two brothers. The book explores the reasons kids join gangs. It shows how members of both gangs are alike underneath. In the end, Ponyboy learns he does not have to stay an outsider.

When it first appeared, *The Outsiders* got mixed reactions. Some people were upset because the book talked about gang violence and drug abuse. Others praised it for its realism.

But the strength of the book is in the depth of its characters. Susan says none of the characters is based on a single person. They are all bits and pieces of people she has known. But they are very real to her. She once said she would not be surprised to see Ponyboy walk in the door. He is that real to her. She begins her books with a character in mind and tries to show how he or she grows.

Susan was 16 when she finished *The Outsiders*. She showed the book to a friend's mother who was an author. The mother liked it. She gave Susan the name of her agent. The book was published the next year.

The book was written from a boy's viewpoint. Susan was afraid people would not read it if they knew the author was a girl. So, she wrote under the name S.E. Hinton.

The book was a huge success. Over a million copies were sold the first year alone. The money Susan made from the sales allowed her to go to college. She entered the University of Tulsa. There she planned to study writing.

But Susan found her sudden fame to be too much. She developed a bad case of writer's block. For four years she could not write at all. She couldn't even use the typewriter to write a letter. She nearly failed her creative writing course. She simply could not write under pressure.

So Susan changed her major to education. She did her student teaching. But she decided she wasn't cut out to be a teacher. She just couldn't stop worrying about the students she taught.

Her boyfriend, David Inhofe, helped her get over her writer's block. He refused to take her out at night unless she had written two pages during the day. Slowly, over several months, Susan wrote her second book. *That Was Then, This Is Now* is a story of drugs and tough kids. The book was published in 1971. Susan and David had married in 1970.

Susan's third book, *Rumble Fish*, was published in 1975. She got the idea for the book from a photograph of a boy on a motorcycle.

Her next book was *Tex*. She wrote *Tex* in 1979. Three years later, it was made into a movie starring Matt Dillon. Later, Dillon also starred in the movies of *The Outsiders* and *Rumble Fish*.

In 1985, *That Was Then, This Is Now* was made into a movie. In the same year, Fox television used *The Outsiders* as the basis for a TV series.

Taming the Star Runner was Hinton's fifth book. She wrote it in 1988 when her son Nick was four. After that she took a seven-year break from writing. She said, "I simply didn't have a story I wanted to tell."

Susan wrote her next book in 1994. It was a picture book for very young children called *Big David, Little David*. Also, she wrote *The Puppy Sister* in 1995.

Susan writes more than books. She writes the screenplays for her novels. She writes television scripts and ads.

When she is not writing, she loves to ride her horse. She also enjoys cooking and spending time with family and friends. She says these things "keep (her) in touch with reality."

Many young people ask Susan for advice about being a writer. She tells them that first they must read everything they can. If you read a lot, after awhile you begin to know good sentence structure, plot, and style.

She recommends reading, then practicing writing. Susan herself wrote for eight years before writing *The Outsiders*. She also advises writing for yourself. She says, "If you don't want to read it, nobody else is going to read it."

Susan writes about teens because she finds them more interesting than adults. Teens are interesting because they are changing so rapidly. As they do, their ideals are tested and they must learn to compromise. Susan is able to show how teenagers feel about what they are going through. She once said, "Ponyboy is how I felt at 14." Apparently, millions of other teens relate to him too.

Susan Hinton is thought of by many as the most successful writer for middle and high school readers. Many young people who do not enjoy reading like to read her books. Librarians say that Susan's books are checked out by teens who normally refuse to read anything not required by a teacher.

Why do teens relate so well to Susan's books? The books mirror the real world. At the same time, they show the idealism of youth. The characters are realistic people facing real problems. Susan often says she herself has the soul of a 15-year-old boy.

Susan Hinton's first book, written when she was 16, created a writing category called "young adult literature." Her books are powerful and real. Many other writers have tried to copy her style. Some have been successful writing young adult books. But there is only one S.E. Hinton.

Getting the Facts

1. Where and in what year was Susan Hinton born?

2. What were the two gangs in *The Outsiders* called?

3. Why were many people upset by the book *The Outsiders*?

4. Why did Susan write as "S.E. Hinton"?

5. Why did Susan change her major from writing to education?

6. Name two other books written by S.E. Hinton.

    (a)

    (b)

7. What advice does Susan give to those who want to become writers?

8. Why does she prefer to write about teens instead of adults?

9. What age group does Susan write for?

10. What new category of literature did Susan create?

Understanding the Story

11. Librarians say that young people who are reluctant to read will check out S.E. Hinton's books. Why do you think they enjoy her books so much?

12. How do you think S.E. Hinton's childhood prepared her to write the type of book she writes?

Getting the Main Idea

In what way do you think young adult literature, as pioneered by S.E. Hinton, can make a contribution in the lives of today's teens?

Applying What You've Learned

S.E. Hinton begins her books by coming up with a character whose story she can tell. Write a paragraph describing an interesting character you could use as the foundation for a book. It should not be one recognizable person, but rather a combination of many people.

Midori
Violinist

As a child of two, Midori discovered the musical instrument that would shape her life. Her mother, Setsu Goto, was a professional violinist. Midori loved to listen to her mother rehearse. When Setsu would leave the room, Midori would climb onto the piano bench. She wanted to touch the violin her mother had put out of reach. She longed to make beautiful music herself. But, after all, Setsu's violin was worth $20,000!

On her third birthday, Midori got her wish. Her mother gave her a tiny violin of her own. Midori's musical talent was by this time already clear. As a two-year-old she had been able

Midori

to hum a Bach concerto after hearing her mother rehearse it. It was time for Setsu to begin giving her talented child violin lessons.

Midori doesn't remember those early lessons. She later said that learning the violin was like learning to walk or talk. "It was a natural thing. It isn't like there's me and then there's the violin. The violin is me."

Midori was born October 25, 1971, in Osaka, Japan. (Her full name is Midori Goto, but she uses only her first name.) Her father was an engineer. Her parents divorced when Midori was very young.

Midori gave her first public recital when she was six years old. At home, she practiced hour after hour. Never did her mother have to prod her. Midori loved to practice. She also went with her mother to the concert hall for rehearsals. Her mother would practice on stage with the symphony. Sometimes Midori listened. Other times she practiced on her own in one of the hall's empty rooms. She progressed rapidly through more and more difficult works.

One day an American friend of Setsu's overheard Midori playing. She was amazed at eight-year-old Midori's skill. She offered to make a tape of Midori playing and take it to the United States. Setsu found a tape recorder. She held it on her lap as Midori played. As the family's two dogs barked in the background, Midori played several difficult pieces flawlessly.

Setsu's friend took the tape to Dorothy Delay. She was a world-famous music teacher at Juilliard School of Music in New York City. Delay was astonished at Midori's extraordinary performance. She offered Midori a scholarship to come to the 1981 Aspen (Colorado) Music Festival. Delay and other world-class musicians were teachers and participants in the festival.

The Aspen Music Festival was Midori's musical debut in the United States. At the festival, Midori played a difficult piece perfectly. Delay knew that she had been right about Midori. The girl was a remarkable prodigy. Later in the festival, Midori played for the class of master violinists. Pinchas Zukerman, one of Midori's idols, heard her play. Her music brought tears to his eyes. "A Midori comes along once in 50 or 75 years," he said. "Ladies and gentlemen, I don't know about you, but I've just witnessed a miracle."

The next year Setsu Goto gave up her career in Japan. She and Midori moved to New York City. Midori began studying at Juilliard.

Midori began giving public performances. She appeared with the New York Philharmonic Orchestra when she was 11. For that performance she received a standing ovation. She also performed for President Reagan at the White House. She began working with an agent, Lee Lamont of ICM Artists. He carefully limited the number of concert appearances she would make in a year.

At the same time, Midori attended the nearby Professional Children's School. Although the school offered standard school subjects and a normal school schedule, it also allowed her to study by correspondence when she went on tour. She was allowed to mail her assignments back and forth to her teachers. (In this manner, Midori later finished high school.)

In 1985, she went to Japan with the European Youth Orchestra, conducted by Leonard Bernstein. The concert was a memorial to the 50th anniversary of the bombing of Hiroshima. She did other concerts that year in Greece, Austria, Germany, Hong Kong, and Canada. She also did a nationwide tour of the United States.

In 1986, 14-year-old Midori made a now legendary performance. It was a hot, humid July night at the Tanglewood Music Festival. Midori was appearing as a guest soloist with the Boston Symphony Orchestra under Leonard Bernstein. She was playing her favorite violin, one that was slightly smaller than normal.

Midori was playing a long, difficult passage of Bernstein's "Serenade." Suddenly, the E-string on her violin snapped. Calmly, Midori put her violin down. She walked over to the concertmaster and borrowed his instrument. She continued playing. Unbelievably, the E-string on that violin broke as well. Midori picked up a third violin and finished the performance without a mistake.

At the end of the performance, the audience went wild. The next day, the story made the front page of *The New York Times*. Midori was surprised by all the fuss. She explained that she borrowed the two violins because she didn't want to stop playing. "Serenade" was a piece that she loved. That performance was a turning point in her career. She won instant fame across the country.

Midori began increasing the number of her concert appearances. In May 1987, she played with the London Symphony Orchestra. Then she flew back to New York for her final exams in school. After that she flew to Japan for several more performances. All summer she played in music festivals around the country. At a festival in New York City, she played two duets with her longtime idol, Pinchas Zukerman.

Midori continued playing as a soloist with many of the world's top orchestras. Critics raved about her performances. In October 1989, Midori made her debut at Carnegie Hall in New York City. The performance was sold-out. The concert was recorded for home-video release.

By 1990, Midori was making as many as 90 appearances a year. She played on the great concert stages of Europe, North America, and the Far East.

In 1992, Midori became concerned that arts education had been eliminated from the New York public schools. She knew that many children would no longer be able to learn about music. Since she loved music as a child, she wanted other children to have a chance to have the same experience.

So, she created Midori and Friends in 1992. The purpose of this group is to bring the performing arts, especially music, into the everyday lives of children. Midori organized a series of five "Adventure Concerts" per year. Musicians come to the schools to perform classical music and jazz. Midori herself has played in 40 public schools as part of this free music education program. For many children, this is their first exposure to fine music.

Midori and Friends also sponsors an instrument instruction program and a new series of after-school family concerts. She devotes much time to this organization. She also performs. And she arranges for other well-known musicians to take part.

Midori loves her new country, America. Now in her twenties, she speaks English fluently (and is somewhat less comfortable with Japanese). She lives in a New York City apartment with her two dogs. Also, she attends New York University.

Midori was one of the most-watched child prodigies of her time. Music critics wondered if she would grow into a mature artist or lose her dedication to music. But Midori has grown with her music into a mature, world-class performer.

When she appears on stage, she enchants the audience with her graceful beauty. Barely five feet tall, she looks tiny and fragile. But when she begins to play, the sounds she makes are incredible. As she plays, she sways to the music, hair flying. As Pinchas Zukerman once said, "When you see her face, you know you're listening to her soul."

Remembering the Facts

1. Why did Midori love the violin from an early age?

2. Who was Midori's first violin teacher?

3. How did Dorothy Delay of New York learn of Midori's talent?

4. Where did Midori make her American debut?

5. Why did Midori and her mother move to New York City?

6. Why was Midori's 1986 performance at Tanglewood legendary?

7. Why did Midori start Midori and Friends?

8. Name three things Midori and Friends does.

   (a)

   (b)

   (c)

Understanding the Story

9. Why do you think Midori's agent wanted to limit the number of performances she did when she was very young?

10. Why do you think many child prodigies do not develop into mature adult musicians?

Getting the Main Idea

Why do you think it is important for children to have the arts as part of their elementary education?

Applying What You've Learned

Write a paragraph describing an experience with the arts which you especially enjoyed. It could be music, dance, theater, or visual art.

Ryan White
AIDS Spokesperson

In 1981, an unwelcome visitor found its way to the United States. It was AIDS, a disease with no known cure. For the first few years, AIDS was a mystery. What caused it? How did it spread? No one had any answers. But everyone was afraid.

It was during this time of panic that 13-year-old Ryan White discovered that he had AIDS. It was his battle with the disease that taught Americans the facts about AIDS and compassion for its victims.

Ryan White was born in Kokomo, Indiana, on December 6, 1971. He lived there with his mother, Jeanne, and younger sister, Andrea. His parents had divorced when the children were very young.

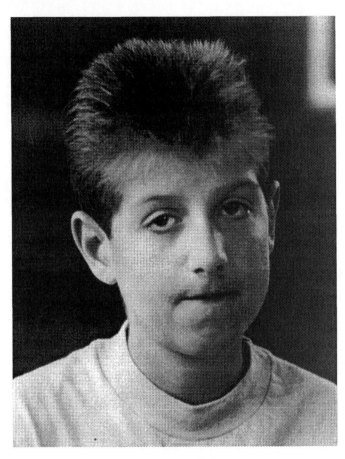

Ryan White

Ryan was born with hemophilia. This is a disorder in which a person's blood does not clot normally. Even a small cut keeps on bleeding and bleeding.

To keep him from bleeding so much, Ryan was given blood transfusions with an extra clotting factor. In this way, his blood could clot more normally. It was these many transfusions that allowed Ryan to enjoy a nearly normal childhood. Without the clotting factor, he would have spent much time in the hospital.

In 1985, shortly before his 13th birthday, Ryan became ill. The doctors discovered that Ryan had AIDS. He had gotten it from one of the blood transfusions meant to save his life.

A few months later, Ryan was feeling better. He began to think about going back to school. But the people of Kokomo panicked. They were afraid their children would catch AIDS from Ryan. Even the teachers did not want Ryan in their classes.

These people did not understand that AIDS could not be spread by casual contact with a victim. The virus cannot be spread through the air, by touch, or by saliva.

The AIDS virus lives in a person's blood. It can be spread by having sex with someone who has the virus. Using a hypodermic needle contaminated with the virus can give a person the virus. A transfusion of contaminated blood can spread the virus.

His classmates were not in danger from Ryan. But no one would listen to reason. Ryan was expelled from school. He had to continue his education using a telephone hookup with the classroom.

Ryan was unhappy with this setup. He missed his friends. He hated being at home alone all day. As Ryan said, "All I wanted to do was to go to school and fit in."

Ryan's mother took the school district to court. She won her case. The judge ordered the school to allow Ryan to return. But he couldn't force the teachers or students to be kind to Ryan.

Ryan returned to eighth grade. It was not a happy reunion. Many parents refused to send their children to school with Ryan. They started their own school somewhere else. The students who stayed at school kept far away from Ryan. No one would sit near him, eat lunch with him, or talk to him.

Other people were openly hostile. Ryan was called terrible names. People threw eggs at the family's car and slashed the tires. When a bullet was shot through the living room window, Jeanne White had enough. She decided the family would have to move.

In the meantime, the happenings in Kokomo had attracted the attention of the news media. It wasn't long before the Ryan White story was headline news across the country. By this time everyone in the country had heard of the Whites' problems.

So, when the Whites moved 25 miles away to Cicero, Indiana, they weren't sure how welcome they would be there, either. But the people of Cicero made Ryan welcome.

When the school leaders in Cicero found out the Whites were coming, they wanted to help Ryan. They required each student to attend an AIDS-awareness seminar. They sent home material on AIDS for the parents to read. By the time the Whites arrived, the town was ready. They welcomed the family. Ryan was able to enter school and make new friends.

In many ways Ryan had a typical teen life in Cicero. He dated girls. He attended the prom. He worked at a skateboard shop. He listened to music on his stereo system. And he had a great car. It was a red Mustang convertible given to him by Michael Jackson.

Ryan tried to live like an average teenager. But his illness had thrust him into the limelight. He was asked to speak on television and at meetings. Ryan was shy and would rather have lived a quiet life. But he knew he could help other people with AIDS.

So, with great courage, Ryan began to speak out. He talked about AIDS and how it is spread. He asked that its victims be treated with compassion. Ryan directed his message to other teenagers. He felt they would listen and understand. He also hoped that by teaching others about AIDS, other children with AIDS would be better treated than he had been.

Ryan appeared on many television talk shows. He gave interviews to magazine and newspaper reporters. He spoke at meetings. He even spoke at a White House hearing on AIDS.

By this time, many movie stars and singers were becoming involved in the AIDS cause. Singer Elton John was one of the first to offer his friendship and support to the White family. Soon after Ryan learned he had AIDS, the singer flew in to visit him. Later he flew all the Whites out to Disneyland for a vacation. Ryan and Elton John became good friends.

Singer Michael Jackson and diver Greg Louganis also became good friends of Ryan's. In 1987, Louganis gave Ryan one of his gold medals from the Pan American games. Ryan met a long list of other public figures and stars.

But Ryan preferred to be treated like anyone else. He picked his public appearances with care. In 1988, he agreed to do an episode for kids about AIDS for the television show *3-2-1 Contact*. The show told about the workings of the AIDS virus. It also told Ryan's story and his feelings about his illness. The show, "I Have AIDS—A Teen-ager's Story," was viewed in schools across the country.

Later, a television movie was produced about Ryan's life. It was called *The Ryan White Story*. In the movie, Ryan played the part of another AIDS patient. Ryan also wrote his autobiography. It is called *Ryan White: My Life Story*.

During the five years since he had been diagnosed with AIDS, Ryan was in and out of the hospital many times. At times, things would look bad, but he would recover and go on with his life.

In September of his senior year in high school, his body began to fail. On April 8, 1990, Ryan died.

Fifteen hundred people attended Ryan's funeral. Family, friends, and celebrities came to honor the memory of the coura-geous teen. Elton John sang a hymn and his song "Skyline Pigeon." This song tells of a bird soaring toward freedom.

Ryan's mother, Jeanne, has continued the work that Ryan began. She lobbied for a bill called the Ryan White Care Bill. This bill was passed in 1990 and renewed in 1996. It provides money for medical care for AIDS patients.

Ryan White accomplished a lot in his short life. He played a major role in changing people's attitudes toward AIDS and its victims. He helped teach millions of people the facts about AIDS. His courage in the face of illness and discrimination is a lesson to us all.

As President George Bush said, "Ryan has helped us understand the truth about AIDS. And he's shown all of us the strength and bravery of the human heart."

Remembering the Facts

1. In what year was AIDS first found in the U.S.?

2. Why did Ryan White need many blood transfusions as a child?

3. Name 3 ways in which the AIDS virus is spread.

   (a)

   (b)

   (c)

4. Why were the people in Kokomo so afraid of Ryan?

5. In what ways did Ryan live a normal teen life?

6. Why did Ryan decide to speak out about AIDS?

7. What is the Ryan White Care Bill?

8. Name two things Ryan accomplished in his lifetime.

   (a)

   (b)

Understanding the Story

9. What do you think made the difference between the attitudes in Kokomo and in Cicero?

10. In what ways is the discrimination against AIDS victims like that against other minorities?

Getting the Main Idea

In what ways do you think Ryan White made things better for other AIDS victims?

Applying What You've Learned

Imagine that you are a student in Ryan White's school in 1985. You have read the facts about how AIDS is spread. Describe your feelings about being in school with Ryan. (Remember that AIDS is very new at this time. Many people are afraid.)

Trevor Ferrell
Activist for the Homeless

It was a cold night in December of 1983. Mr. and Mrs. Ferrell were enjoying a quiet cup of coffee. Their four children were all happily playing in another part of the house. The Ferrells were content in their warm, cozy, suburban world.

Suddenly, 11-year-old Trevor burst into the room. "The TV had these pictures of people who were living on the street!" he exclaimed. "Do people really live like that . . . in America?"

His father replied that there were many homeless people even in their own city of Philadelphia. Trevor couldn't believe it. How could people have no place to sleep, no home? How could they stay alive with no blankets?

Trevor Ferrell

Trevor insisted that his parents take him downtown. He planned to give his own blanket and pillow to a homeless person. His parents were not thrilled with that idea. They were tired from a long day of work. But Trevor was so persistent, they finally gave in.

Downtown Philadelphia was 12 miles from their home in the suburbs. As soon as they arrived in the city center, they saw a man sleeping on a grate on the street corner. Steam from the subway below rose through the grate, providing some warmth. But the man had no protection from the fierce wind.

Trevor got out of the car. He approached the sleeping man. "Here, sir, here's a blanket for you." Trevor handed the man the blanket and pillow. The man looked dazed. "Thank you very much. God bless you," he answered.

The Ferrells did not know it at the time, but that night was the beginning of a big change in their lives.

The next day, when Mr. Ferrell came home from work, he was greeted at the door by Trevor. "Can we go again tonight? Mom and I found two more blankets," the boy said. So that night Trevor gave two more blankets to the homeless.

The Ferrells kept going downtown three or four nights a week. They took coats, blankets, and sweaters each time. Soon they had given away all the spare items they had in the house.

Trevor decided they would have to get others to help. He wanted to make posters to put up. His mother was glad to see him trying to write something by himself. Trevor had dyslexia. That is a reading disability, and it made school hard for him.

Trevor worked hard on his poster. He told the story of how he was trying to bring blankets to the homeless. His dad made copies of the poster and put them up. He put Trevor's photo on the top right-hand corner.

People saw the posters and began bringing in coats and blankets. One person donated a blue Volkswagen van. The Ferrells hung a clothes rack in the van. Trevor hung the coats. Then people could choose a coat they liked.

Trevor thought they could get more donations if they put an ad in the newspaper. His mother drove him to the newspaper office. Trevor went in by himself and talked to a reporter. She was very interested in his story and promised to help.

The reporter came with Trevor on one of his downtown trips. Her story appeared just after Christmas in the local paper. Then it was picked up by the television stations. Soon Trevor's story was in *The New York Times* and on all the wire services. Trevor was news all across America.

Cash, checks, and donations poured in. Other people volunteered to help. By March, the Ferrells were going downtown every night.

Some people thought the Ferrells were crazy. At school, some of Trevor's classmates teased him. At recess, some hit him and asked him if he had any blankets for them. Trevor kept all this to himself. The teasing hurt. But he believed in what he was doing.

One night on the drive downtown, Trevor noticed there were a lot of houses standing empty. He wondered why they couldn't get one of these empty houses as a home for the street people to live in.

A few weeks later, the Ferrells got a call from the Peace Mission Movement. They had an old hotel they were willing to donate to the homeless. The house had 33 bedrooms and 19 bathrooms. But it had stood empty for three years. It would take a lot of work to make it livable.

This is how Trevor's Place—A Home for the Homeless got its start. It was March 16, 1984. It had been less than three months since Trevor handed his blanket to that first homeless man. A simple act of concern had blossomed into a full-time job for the entire family. The family named this work "Trevor's Campaign."

There was a lot of work to do before the building would be livable. For weeks, teams of 10 to 20 volunteers spent their weekends cleaning and repairing the old house. Without the volunteers, the plumbing repairs would have cost $20,000. Someone donated a stove. Now the kitchen could be used.

Trevor's Place had three goals. It would provide a place of warmth and safety and a "family" to belong to. It would give those who were able to work some kind of job training. Then it would help them find jobs.

The Ferrell family paid a price for their work. Mr. Ferrell closed his electronics shop. He began to work full-time for the Campaign. Trevor began falling behind in school. And Mrs. Ferrell was tired from hard work and lack of rest. But as Trevor's Place opened its doors, they felt it had all been worth it.

Before long, there were hundreds of volunteers working with the Campaign. Some people took hot meals to the homeless. Others delivered clothing. Others gave donations of money. All had caught Trevor's spirit of concern for humanity.

As one volunteer said, "This child named Trevor has led the way. We can all make our lives worthwhile by being willing to see others' needs and then doing something about it. . . . Whatever we give of ourselves, it helps to . . . add meaning to our lives here."

Trevor was accepted and loved by the street people. He never judged anyone or asked questions about how they happened to be homeless. He simply accepted them as they were. And they responded to that. Trevor always felt he gained as much from knowing the street people as they gained from his gifts.

Trevor's actions are a challenge to those who think that one person can't make a difference. Trevor and his family are making a difference, and inspiring others to do the same. People are beginning to realize that personal commitment can be an answer to some of the world's problems. As Trevor said, "I am only one, but I am one. I can't do everything, but I can do something."

Trevor's actions have touched the hearts of people around the world. He was awarded the John Rogers Integrity Award in 1984. This honor was also given to Mother Teresa and Gandhi. He also went to the White House, where he received a commendation from President Reagan in 1985. The Philadelphia City Council passed a resolution praising Trevor as "an example of the good that lies in the human heart."

Trevor appeared on TV talk shows. He gave interviews to magazine and newspaper reporters from around the world.

Yet the recognition that meant the most to him came from within. Trevor most appreciated the looks of thanks from those who had no hope, and notes such as this one from an unknown man:

"Last night, in my loneliness, poverty, and utter despair, I could have ended it all. It was freezing cold and pouring rain. I had reached the dregs of human suffering, having lost both my wife and son. After I had long since given up, there I was, a street person. Suddenly, there in front of me stood a little boy who gave me a respectful, 'Here sir, I have a blanket for you.' He had given me more than a blanket, he gave me new hope. I fell in love with that little boy named Trevor and at the same time I fell in love again with life."

Today, Trevor's Campaign continues in Philadelphia. Trevor's Place provides shelter for the homeless. After more hard work, the Campaign bought Trevor's Next Door, the building next door to Trevor's Place. It is a home for women and children that provides 24-hour day care along with social and educational programs.

Today, Trevor and his family have another dream. They are working on a project to help inner-city youth. It is called Trevor's Youth Farm School. The program's goal is to show troubled youth a better way to live than with gangs and drugs.

Trevor and his family also run two Trevor's Thrift Shops. They sell donated clothes, furniture, and appliances. Profits from the shops are going to help fund Trevor's Youth Farm School. Profits from the sales of the Ferrells' book (*Trevor's Place—The Story of the Boy Who Brings Hope to the Homeless*) also go to fund Trevor's Youth Farm School.

Despite his youth, Trevor Ferrell found a way to offer light to people who lived in the dark world of homelessness. He showed that one person, no matter how young, could make a difference. One of Trevor's favorite quotes (from John Bunyan) tells the story of his life: "You have not lived today until you have done something for someone who can never repay you."

Remembering the Facts

1. How did Trevor Ferrell first learn about the homeless?

2. What did he do when he learned there were homeless people in his city?

3. Trevor had dyslexia. What does that mean?

4. How did Trevor get more people to bring coats and blankets?

5. How did Trevor become known all across the country?

6. How were some children in Trevor's school unkind to him?

7. How did Trevor's Place get started?

8. Name two ways in which the Campaign was hard on the Ferrells.

    (a)

    (b)

9. Why did the street people accept and love Trevor?

10. Name an award Trevor received.

Understanding the Story

11. What do you think are some of the reasons a person might become homeless?

12. In what ways do people benefit from doing volunteer work?

Getting the Main Idea

What do you think are the most important lessons we can all learn from Trevor's story?

Applying What You've Learned

Write a paragraph telling of the needs you see in your own community. How do you think one person could make a difference with one of these needs?

Samantha Smith
Ambassador

It was not war. Yet it was not peace. It was called the Cold War between the United States and the Soviet Union. It lasted over 40 years, from the mid-1940's until the end of the 1980's.

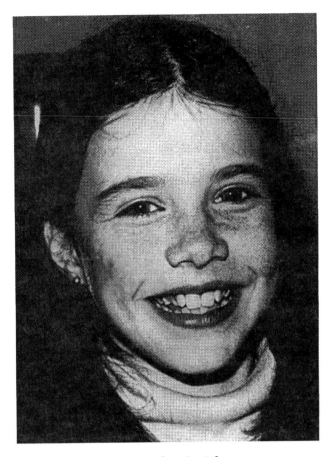

Samantha Smith

During World War II, America and the Soviet Union fought on the same side. But after the war, their alliance ended. The communist Soviets began taking over Eastern European countries. Soon many countries were under communist rule.

The Western powers, led by the United States, opposed the spread of communism. The Eastern powers, led by the Soviet Union, wanted to spread communism. Soon many countries were allied with either the East or the West.

The two sides began an arms race. They tried to outdo each other in making bigger, more powerful nuclear weapons. It was a tense time. Everyone worried that the Cold War might become a "hot" war at any moment. Each side feared being wiped out with the touch of a button.

A 10-year-old girl named Samantha Smith took action. She wrote a letter to the Soviet leader, Yuri Andropov, asking for peace. His answer resulted in her trip to the Soviet Union. There she brought about better understanding on both sides.

Samantha Smith was born on June 29, 1972, in Houlton, Maine. When Samantha was in the third grade, she and her parents moved to Manchester, Maine.

Samantha was a friendly and caring girl. What she saw on the television news bothered her. Every night there was something about missiles or nuclear bombs. On one show, a scientist explained how a nuclear war would destroy earth. No one would win a nuclear war.

Samantha was worried. So she decided to do something about it. The fifth-grade girl wrote a letter to Yuri Andropov in November 1982. She wrote:

Dear Mr. Andropov,

My name is Samantha Smith. I am ten years old. Congratulations on your new job. I have been worrying about Russia and the United States getting into a nuclear war. Are you going to vote to have a war or not? If you aren't please tell me how you are going to help to not have a war. This question you do not have to answer, but I would like to know why you want to conquer the world or at least our country. God made the world for us to live together in peace and not to fight.

Sincerely,

Samantha Smith

Four or five months went by. Samantha had nearly forgotten about the letter. One day a reporter from United Press International called Samantha. She wanted to know if Samantha had really written a letter to Yuri Andropov.

An article about Samantha's letter had been printed in the Soviet newspaper *Pravda.* The letter had been printed as well. The article did not answer Samantha's questions. It said that she could be excused for her misunderstanding of the Soviet people since she was only 10.

Samantha was not happy with the article. She felt she deserved an answer to her questions even though she was a child. So she wrote a letter to the Soviet ambassador in Washington, D.C. Ambassador Dobrynin was the official Soviet representative to the United States. Samantha hoped Dobrynin could get Andropov to answer her letter.

It worked! Soon Samantha received a letter from Andropov himself. He said that her question was "the most important of those that every thinking man can pose. . . . We in the Soviet Union are trying to do everything so that there will not be war between our countries. We want peace for ourselves and for all peoples of the planet. For our children and for you, Samantha. . . . ." He then invited Samantha to come visit the Soviet Union.

Suddenly, Samantha was famous. TV and newspapers from around the world began calling for interviews. Even reporters from the Soviet Union showed up. Soviets wanted to know more about the girl who had written to the Russian leader.

On July 7, 1983, Samantha and her parents left for the Soviet Union. Crowds of reporters and photographers saw them off.

They arrived in Moscow nine hours later. They were met by two guides who would help them on their two-week stay. Samantha enjoyed sightseeing in Moscow. She met important government leaders. Andropov did not have time to see her, but he sent gifts.

Later, Samantha stayed for a few days at the Young Pioneer Camp at Artek. Nearly 4,000 of the brightest, most talented Soviet students were at the camp for a month. Samantha stayed in the girls' dorm. She became friends with several of the girls.

The Soviet students had many questions about America. They were especially interested in American clothes and music. None of them hated America. Samantha said, "If we could be friends by just getting to know each other, then what are our countries really arguing about?"

After leaving the camp, Samantha visited a collective farm. The farm was owned by the government. A group of people lived and worked on the farm together.

Later, she spent a few days in Leningrad. The family did some sightseeing and enjoyed the ballet. Then it was back to Moscow for more sightseeing. Everywhere she went, Samantha was followed by a mob of reporters. The little girl charmed everyone she met with her happy smile and her enthusiasm.

Samantha returned home to Maine. But her peace mission was not over. She wrote a book called *Journey to the Soviet Union*. It is filled with pictures of her trip to the Soviet Union. In it, Samantha says, "The world seems not so complicated as it did when I looked at travel books from the library. And the people of the world seem more like people in my own neighborhood. I think they are more like me than I ever realized."

Samantha also gave interviews to newspaper and television reporters. She wanted everyone to know about the friendly people she had met in the Soviet Union.

In January 1984, Samantha went to Japan. She was the keynote speaker for the Children's International Symposium. People in Japan called her the "Angel of Peace."

Samantha liked traveling to talk about peace. Her father gave up his teaching job to travel with her. She hosted a 90-minute television show in which she interviewed presidential candidates. She appeared on other talk shows.

Samantha was offered a role in a new television show. It was called *Lime Street*. She loved acting, although it meant she had to be away from home a lot.

The fourth episode of *Lime Street* was filmed in England in September of 1985. Samantha's father went with her. On the way home, their plane crashed only 30 miles from home. All eight people on board, including Samantha and her father, were killed.

Samantha Smith was only 13 years old when she died. But she had reached her goal of making people think about peace. More than 1,000 people came to her funeral. Both President Reagan and the new Soviet leader, Mikhail Gorbachev, wrote sympathy letters to Samantha's mother.

In 1989, the Cold War ended. The once mighty Soviet Union broke into many separate countries.

The Soviets have not forgotten Samantha Smith. They named a flower, a star, and a children's center after her. In Augusta, Maine, a statue was erected in Samantha's honor. It shows a young girl with a dove (a peace symbol) and a bear (the symbol of the Soviet Union).

Samantha's mother set up the Samantha Smith Foundation. It sponsors exchange students between America and countries that were once part of the Soviet Union. She hopes to continue her daughter's work of promoting understanding between people of different nations—work that began with one heartfelt letter.

Remembering the Facts

1. When did the Cold War take place?

2. What was the arms race?

3. Why was Samantha worried about the arms race?

4. What did *Pravda* say about Samantha's letter to Andropov?

5. What did Samantha do when Andropov did not answer her letter?

6. When Andropov finally answered, what did he say?

7. What interested Soviet students most about American students?

8. How did Samantha keep working for peace when she came home?

9. Name two ways in which the Soviets honored Samantha.

   (a)

   (b)

10. What is the purpose of the Samantha Smith Foundation?

Understanding the Story

11. People often feel helpless to change the course of world events. How do you think Samantha Smith showed people around the world that they could make a difference?

12. Do you think Samantha's age made her a more effective ambassador? Why or why not?

Getting the Main Idea

Samantha died at age 13. Do you think that Samantha had reached her goal of making people think about peace? Why or why not?

Applying What You've Learned

Imagine that Samantha were still alive. Write a paragraph telling about an issue you think she would be concerned about.

Oscar De La Hoya
Boxer

The barrio of East Los Angeles is not an easy place to grow up. There are run-down apartment buildings. There's graffiti on the walls. Street gangs control their turf. There are drug dealers, violence, and guns. In such a place, many young boys join gangs because gangs give them a place to belong, a sense of safety.

Oscar De La Hoya was born in the barrio of East L.A., a section of the city that is predominantly Spanish-speaking. But he stayed away from gangs. Instead, he channeled his energy into boxing. He fought his way out of the barrio, winning an Olympic gold medal in 1992 and the World Boxing Council (WBC) super-lightweight belt in 1996.

Oscar De La Hoya

Oscar De La Hoya was born on February 4, 1973. His parents, Joel and Cecilia De La Hoya, came to Los Angeles from Mexico. Joel De La Hoya was a professional boxer. But after his three children were born, he worked as a clerk in an air-conditioning business. Cecilia worked as a seamstress. Although both parents worked hard, there was little money in the family.

As a child, Oscar liked to ride his skateboard. He also enjoyed drawing. His friends were his favorite drawing subjects. By the age of six, many of Oscar's friends had already joined gangs. They wanted Oscar to join too, but he refused. Because he was not part of their group, gang members picked fights with Oscar.

By the time he was six years old, Oscar was tired of losing fights. He went with his father to the neighborhood gym to learn how to box. From the very first day, Oscar loved boxing.

Joel De La Hoya made sure that Oscar trained at the gym every day. The sport came naturally to Oscar. As a seven-year-old, Oscar won his first fight. He began winning trophies. He also won money. The men of the neighborhood gave dollar bills to the boys who won their fights. Now the boys in the neighborhood gangs no longer wanted to fight Oscar. He was too good!

When Oscar was 11 years old, he watched another East L.A. fighter on television. Paul Gonzales won the gold medal at the 1984 Olympics. Gonzales became a hero for Oscar, and for many Hispanic Americans in East L.A.

From that point on, Oscar De La Hoya knew exactly what he wanted to do with his life. He began working with a trainer, Robert Alcazar. He followed his dream with a single-minded dedication. Oscar used what he calls his "D formula." Oscar says, "My 3 D's are dedication, discipline, and desire." The D formula worked! At age 15, Oscar became the Junior Olympic champion in the 119-pound class. The next year, he won the national Golden Gloves title in the 125-pound class.

In 1990, at age 17, Oscar De La Hoya won the U.S. amateur boxing championship. Also that year, he won the gold medal at the Goodwill Games in Seattle. Both of these wins were in the 125-pound class. During his amateur career, Oscar fought 228 matches and lost only 5!

Oscar kept up with his schoolwork as well. He was a student at Garfield High School. This tough barrio school was made famous in the movie *Stand and Deliver* starring Edward James Olmos. When he was on the road on the boxing circuit, Oscar had a tutor to help him with his assignments. He graduated right on schedule in June 1991.

In the meantime, Oscar's mother had been ill with cancer. She died at the age of 38, shortly after Oscar won the Goodwill Games in 1990. Cecilia De La Hoya had been Oscar's biggest fan. The two were very close. Just before she died, she told Oscar that her dream was for him to win an Olympic gold medal.

In 1992, two years after his mother died, Oscar went to the Olympic games in Barcelona, Spain. He had trained hard and made the U.S. Olympic team in the 132-pound weight class.

In the gold-medal round, Oscar fought one of the few boxers who had beaten him before. It meant a lot to Oscar to win that gold medal. But he was not sure he would win. Later, he said that something happened to him in the ring that day. He felt his mother's presence as if she were sitting at ringside. This gave him the confidence he needed.

Oscar won the fight. In fact, he was the only U.S. boxer to win a gold medal at the Olympics that year. He was proud and happy. But the first thing he did after returning home was to go to the cemetery to lay his medal on his mother's grave. "She was my inspiration," he said.

Just three months after the Olympics, Oscar turned pro. He kept on winning professional fights until he had a 21–0 record. Finally he came to what he thought of as his real test. He would fight the World Boxing Council champion, Julio Cesar Chavez. Chavez was 10 years older than Oscar De La Hoya. He was Mexico's most popular boxer, having won 97 of 99 fights. Oscar knew that this fight would be his most difficult.

Oscar trained hard for the fight. He ran six miles a day. He practiced sparring. And he did at least 140 pushups daily to build upper-body strength. Finally, he was ready. The fight did not last long. It was very one-sided. The referee stopped the match two minutes into the fourth round to protect Julio from serious injury. Oscar De La Hoya was the new World Boxing Council super-light-weight champion.

Oscar De La Hoya continued his winning ways. In 1997 he won all five fights he entered. He made the most money a non-heavy-weight fighter has ever made. *Forbes* magazine listed his 1997 winnings as $37 million dollars. Oscar De La Hoya has become the "Golden Boy" of boxing.

Oscar has moved out of the barrio. But he hasn't forgotten his roots. In his wallet, he carries a food stamp to remind him of leaner days. He started the Oscar De La Hoya Foundation to help needy children. In 1996, he paid $500,000 for the rundown gym where he used to train as a boy. He spent another $250,000 to remodel it. Now the gym is known as the Oscar De La Hoya Youth Boxing Center. Oscar hopes it will be a safe haven for kids who want to escape the street gangs as he did.

Oscar De La Hoya has said (in *People Weekly*), "My favorite thing about being a champion is that I can be a role model for kids." He tries to do this in several ways. He has given money to deserving Garfield High students for scholarships. He has donated money to the school for activities.

He also tries to be a good example by the way he acts. Some fighters are mean and use bad language. They yell and brag when they win a fight. But Oscar De La Hoya says his mother raised him to have good manners. He speaks quietly and is respectful of other fighters.

Oscar De La Hoya has said that he plans to retire from boxing by age 28. Then he hopes to go to college to study architecture. In February 1997, he tried out his budding architectural skills. He designed the log cabin where he lives when he trains. The cabin is at Big Bear Lake, California.

In his spare time, Oscar likes to play golf. He likes it so much that he tries to play every day when he's not training for a fight. He also enjoys driving cars, fishing, and playing basketball.

Mild-mannered, clean-cut, and handsome, Oscar De La Hoya has given boxing a new image. He is truly boxing's "Golden Boy."

Remembering the Facts

1. Where was Oscar De La Hoya born?

2. Why did Oscar begin learning to box at age six?

3. Which other Hispanic American fighter was Oscar's hero when he was a boy?

4. What is Oscar's "D formula"?

5. How did Oscar keep up with his classwork at Garfield High when he was on the road so much?

6. What dream did Oscar's mother have for him?

7. Why did Oscar become well known to Americans in 1992?

8. What title did he win by beating Julio Cesar Chavez?

9. Name two ways in which Oscar has helped the youth of his old neighborhood.

   (a)

   (b)

10. What does Oscar plan to do when he retires from boxing?

Understanding the Story

11. In what ways do you think Oscar De La Hoya is different from the typical boxer? In what ways do you think he is the same?

12. Why do you think so many kids in the barrio join gangs?

Getting the Main Idea

How do you think Oscar De La Hoya is a good role model for American youth?

Applying What You've Learned

Imagine that you are a teen living in the barrio of East L.A. Write a paragraph telling how you could resist the pressure to join a street gang.

Tiger Woods
Golfer

Basketball has Michael Jordan. Hockey has Wayne Gretzky. And golf has Tiger Woods. They are the superstars of their sport. But there is more. These players are creating an excitement about their sport as no one else can. Tiger Woods is defining the sport of golf for the 21st century!

In his book *The Tiger Woods Way*, author John Andrisani explains, "Tiger Woods is probably better at golf at 21 than anyone who ever played golf . . . He is Paul Bunyan, Superman, the biblical David and The Incredible Hulk all wrapped up in one. (Some say) that courses aren't big enough for Tiger. That may be an exaggeration. But one thing is for sure. When Tiger

Tiger Woods

stands over a ball, readying himself to drive, the (audience) is filled with . . . excitement. When he finally makes contact, everyone's eyes trace the ball's flight with a look of unparalleled amazement. . . . The great shots he hits are more sensational, more inspiring, and more unbelievable than anything the golf world has ever witnessed."

Eldrick "Tiger" Woods was born December 30, 1975, in Cypress, California. His father, Earl Woods, was a retired army officer. Earl had met his wife Kultida in her native country of Thailand. Earl Woods was serving as a Green Beret there during the Vietnam War.

Earl Woods loved to play golf. And he wasted little time introducing Eldrick to the sport. He propped six-month-old Eldrick up in a high chair so he could watch his dad hit golf balls into a net. When Eldrick was 11 months old, Earl cut a golf club down to size for him. He showed his baby boy how to swing the club. Patiently, he showed him over and over.

By the time Eldrick was two years old, his golf swing looked professional. He earned a spot on *The Mike Douglas Show* on television. To everyone's amazement, he was able to out-putt Bob Hope on the show. Two years later, Eldrick appeared on the TV show *That's Incredible*. Again he showed his ability to out-putt the adult guests on the show. Because of these appearances, Tiger Woods has been followed by the media since he was two.

Earl continued to teach Eldrick about golf. He explained the meaning of golf terms like "set up" and "over the top." Eldrick was an eager pupil. Like other preschool boys, he liked toy cars and trucks. But he really liked playing with golf equipment.

From an early age, Eldrick had a strong will to win. He was fearless when playing a match, even against much older players. Because of this, the boy reminded Earl Woods of a fearless commander he had during the Vietnam War. "He was a tiger on the field (of battle), and my son is a tiger on the course." So, Earl gave his son the nickname "Tiger." The nickname stuck.

Tiger competed in his first junior tournament when he was three. He used special golf clubs cut down to size. By the time Tiger was in kindergarten he was winning the junior tournaments he entered. He regularly beat players who were three times his age.

As Tiger grew older, his love of the game grew. It did not bother him to play against players who were older and played better than he did. He saw this as an opportunity to learn to play better. Tiger practiced whenever he could. During the summer, he played almost every day. He entered many tournaments, often bringing home trophies.

Tiger Woods kept getting better. When Tiger was 11, Earl Woods worked with him, using "boot camp" techniques to make him mentally tough. At the same time, his mother taught him about

Buddhism. This is a religion that uses meditation as a form of prayer. All of these things combined to give Tiger an unusual ability to focus on his game.

In 1991, Tiger Woods won his first U.S. Junior Amateur title. He repeated this feat in 1992 and 1993. Next, he moved to the U.S. Amateur (adult) matches. He won his first U.S. Amateur title in 1994. He was the youngest male ever to do so. He won the title again in 1995 and 1996. No golfer before him had ever won three straight titles at either level.

Tiger enrolled at Stanford University on a full scholarship. He dropped out after his second year to become a professional golfer.

Nineteen hundred ninety-six was his first year as a pro. In October of that year, he won the Las Vegas Invitational. Next he won the Walt Disney Classic. Tiger Woods made the cover of *Sports Illustrated* magazine that year as the 1996 Sportsman of the Year.

Many people wondered if Tiger-mania was for real. But 1997 was an even better year for Tiger. In April, he won the most honored tournament in golf—the Master's Tournament. He set a record for the best score and largest margin of victory ever for the tournament. Of course, he was also the youngest person in history to win the tournament. Most golfers on the pro tour go years without winning a tournament. And most only dream of winning the green jacket that is presented to each winner of the Master's Tournament.

There's no doubt that Tiger Woods is a natural athlete. He has the most powerful drive in the game. He averages 294 yards per drive. This is the longest among all the PGA golfers.

But the real secret of his success is attitude. He is very focused on what he wants to do. He charms his audience with his smile and polite manners, but inside that friendly person lies the fierce heart of a true competitor.

Tiger Woods has built an entire industry on his appeal. He signed a $60 million endorsement deal to do ads for Nike and Titleist (a golf-equipment company). He is working on a line of golf clubs, Nike sportswear and shoes, and a line of watches. He is also doing a $2.2 million book deal with Warner Books. In 1997, *Forbes* magazine reported that Tiger was second only to Michael Jordan in money earned from endorsements. In 1997, he earned a cool $24 million from ads. His golf winnings were another $2.1 million.

Tiger is the only minority golfer ever to win a major tournament. He is one of only two minority golfers on the PGA. Tour. (Tiger is part black and part Asian.) For this reason, some sports-writers have called him "the most important athlete since Jackie Robinson." Fifty years ago, Jackie Robinson was the first black baseball player to play in the major leagues.

Being the first minority golfer to make it big creates a certain amount of pressure for Tiger. But he has accepted this role. Tiger said (in *Boys' Life*), "I've accepted that since I was a very little boy. I like the fact that I can influence people with my game in a positive way."

Tiger hopes that other minority young people will try golf. He and his father have started a foundation to provide clinics and programs for minority young people. About 2,500 young would-be golfers signed up for his first clinic in 1997 in Scottsdale, Arizona. Six other clinics were held later that year at golf courses around the country. Tiger hopes that once young people try golf, they will find out that it's a lot of fun. Certainly Tiger has had a big role in the recent increase in young people and minorities playing golf!

Tiger Woods, at 21, is the biggest superstar of the golf world. He has reached this level of excellence through talent, hard work, and a winning attitude. Tiger Woods is Michael Jordan's only hero! He is a worthy hero and role model to millions of young Americans as well.

Remembering the Facts

1. In what two ways is Tiger Woods like Michael Jordan and Wayne Gretzky?

   (a)

   (b)

2. At what age did Earl Woods introduce his son to golf?

3. Why has Tiger been followed by the media since he was two years old?

4. How did Tiger get his nickname?

5. What two things gave Tiger his unusual ability to concentrate?

   (a)

   (b)

6. What tournament did Tiger win in 1991, 1992, and 1993?

7. What tournament did he win in 1994, 1995, and 1996?

8. What tournament did Tiger win the year he turned pro?

9. How is Tiger making most of his money?

10. How is Tiger helping minority youngsters to learn about golf?

Understanding the Story

11. Why do you think that being the first minority golf star would put pressure on Tiger?

12. Tiger Woods was clearly born with an exceptional athletic talent. What other factors do you think are necessary for an athlete to make it big in a sport?

Getting the Main Idea

Why do you think Tiger Woods is an excellent role model for young Americans?

Applying What You've Learned

At 21, Tiger Woods won golf's most important tournament. Write a paragraph telling what you imagine could be Tiger Woods's greatest challenge in the coming years.

Jason Gaes
Cancer Survivor

"Is Jason going to die?"

"If I am to be honest, I have to tell you . . . probably yes."

These words were spoken by a doctor at the famous Mayo Clinic. They were meant for the parents of six-year-old Jason Gaes.

But Jason did not die. Today he is a healthy teenager. His courage has given hope to many other cancer patients.

Jason Gaes was born on October 12, 1977. He had a twin brother, Tim. An older brother and a younger sister completed the family. The family lived in Worthington, Minnesota.

Jason Gaes

Until he was six, his childhood was a happy one. He went to kindergarten. He played sports. And he played with his brothers and baby sister. The Gaes family was large and close. Grandparents, aunts, uncles, and cousins lived nearby.

When Jason was six, his uncle spotted a black lump in the boy's mouth. His mother took him to the dentist. She thought he would probably need a tooth pulled. The dentist sent Jason to an oral surgeon the next day. The surgeon did pull one of Jason's teeth that was coming in crooked next to the lump. He also examined the lump carefully. He found that the lump was a malignant tumor. Jason had cancer.

Cancer is a disease in which one of the billions of cells in the body develops abnormally. This cell then begins to multiply very quickly. The cells form a mass called a tumor.

Some tumors are benign. That means they do not spread to other areas of the body. A benign tumor can be removed. The patient is then free from disease.

Other tumors are malignant. A malignant tumor means cancer is present. It may grow larger and larger, entering the nearby tissues which contain healthy cells. Or it may grow and divide, forming new tumors. These tumors may spread through the body via the blood or lymph system.

As Jason was waking up from his surgery, he complained of a "bump" in his stomach. The doctor examined Jason. He found a lump the size of a golf ball. The lump was a second tumor.

With this discovery, Jason's parents were terrified. Piling into the car, they drove nearly four hours to the Mayo Clinic. This is a famous hospital in Rochester, Minnesota.

They arrived at 10:00 P.M. In the few hours it had taken to drive there, the tumor in Jason's stomach had grown to the size of a grapefruit. Soon the doctors found four more tumors.

Jason was diagnosed with Burkitt's lymphoma, a rare, fast-growing kind of cancer. Jason was given a one-in-five chance of living.

Over the next two years, Jason underwent many tests and treatments to rid his body of cancer. One treatment was radiation therapy. This treatment beams high-energy X-rays straight at the cancerous cells. It damages or destroys the fast-growing cancer cells. The size of the tumor is reduced this way.

A second kind of treatment was chemotherapy. This means chemical therapy or drug therapy. These drugs go through the entire body via the bloodstream. The goal is to kill other cancer cells that may have spread so they don't form new tumors.

Some of the treatments and tests were painful. Others made Jason throw up. He lost all his hair. He was weak and tired. Between treatments, he had short periods when he felt better.

On days when Jason felt well, he did many things he had enjoyed before he got sick. "If I could say just one thing to kids with cancer," Jason says, "it'd be . . . don't stop doing the things you really love to do." Jason swam and played ball whenever he could.

But the good times did not last long. Soon he would be back in the hospital for more tests and treatment. After six months of treatment, Jason wanted to quit. He felt awful. And he was tired of the painful treatments and the sickness that followed. To keep him going, his mother promised him a huge party at the end of his treatments.

A year later, Jason was still undergoing treatments. When he was in the hospital, many people sent cards, presents, and flowers. One person sent a book about a boy with cancer called *Hang Tough*. Jason was not happy with the end of the book. The boy in the story died.

Jason asked his mother, "Why don't they write about kids who live and grow up?" His mother suggested he could write his own book. Jason didn't answer her. She thought that was the end of it. But six months later, as she was folding clothes, Jason threw a yellow spiral notebook into her lap. "Here's my book," he said.

Jason had decided to write a book that would help other children with cancer. He hoped that some good could come out of all the pain and fear he had gone through.

Jason had begun writing his book by talking into a tape recorder. He pretended he was talking to a boy with cancer. He tried to tell this boy about what would happen to him in the hospital. He talked about how other people would treat him. And he talked about how to think positively. Jason called his book *My book for kids with cansur.*

Jason finished nearly two years of treatments. The reports were good. The doctors found that he was free of cancer! Jason was then eight years old.

Jason's parents threw him the party they had promised. Four hundred people packed the hall at a nearby resort. Friends, relatives, and Jason's doctors and nurses were there.

The party invitations were photocopies of Jason's book. It had been illustrated by Jason's brothers to look like a "real" book.

At the party were some people from the American Cancer Society. They wanted to make copies of the book for other children who had cancer. They thought Jason had done a great job of telling about his experiences so another child could understand.

A local TV station heard about Jason. They did a story about him. A publisher saw the program. He offered to publish the book and donate part of the profits to the American Cancer Society. The book was printed just the way Jason and his brothers created it. Over five million copies of the book have been printed. It has been translated into other languages and sold around the world.

In 1988, Jason was presented with the American Courage Award from President Reagan. Jason thought that was "really neat." But a visit from quarterback Dan Marino ranked "awesome"!

In 1989, HBO made a movie about Jason and his family, called *You Don't Have to Die*. It won an Academy Award for the Live Short Action category. In 1992, the Gaes family published a book called *You Don't Have to Die: One Family's Guide to Surviving Cancer.*

Jason was interviewed on all the major talk shows. Stories about him appeared in many magazines. Jason traveled around the country speaking about cancer. He missed so much school his parents hired a tutor to help him keep up. They also helped him answer the hundreds of letters and phone calls he received every week.

Jason is now 20 years old. He is a college student. He hopes to be a doctor who works with children who have cancer.

Jason's message of hope has reached thousands of kids with cancer. He cared enough to reach out to others who were suffering as he did. As Jason said in his book: "If you get cansur don't be scared cause lots of people get over having cansur and grow up without dying. Like Mike Nelson and Doug Cerny and Vince Varpness and President Reagan and me."

Remembering the Facts

1. What was the first sign there was something wrong with Jason?

2. What is a malignant tumor?

3. What type of cancer did Jason have?

4. How does radiation therapy destroy cancer cells?

5. How does chemotherapy work?

6. What inspired Jason to write his book?

7. What was the purpose of the book?

8. How did the book get published?

9. What movie did HBO make about Jason's story?

10. In what other ways did Jason tell his story?

Understanding the Story

11. How do you think the illness of one person would affect all the members of the family?

12. Jason's mother says the Gaes family is not heroic. She says their story tells of the human will to live and handle a crisis. In what ways do you agree or disagree?

Getting the Main Idea

Jason's book has helped children around the world who have cancer. Why do you think his simple handwritten book could be more helpful than a longer book written by an adult?

Applying What You've Learned

Write a paragraph in which you give information that will help another student through a crisis or problem you have dealt with. For example: moving, death of a loved one, divorce, breaking up with a boyfriend or girlfriend, failing a test, etc.

Vocabulary

Benjamin West: Artist

- Quaker
- classical
- influenced
- prophecy
- portrait
- dominated
- canvas
- miniature
- foretold
- engraving
- colonies
- indigo

Phillis Wheatley: Poet

- abolitionist
- elegy
- obstacles
- pamphlet
- merchant
- pinions
- heritage
- encouraged
- literature

Maria Mitchell: Astronomer

- chronometer
- observations
- opportunity
- sextant
- rote
- capacity
- astronomy
- moralistic
- observatory
- persistence

Allen Jay: Underground Railroad "Conductor"

- plantation
- bluing
- conductor
- religious
- illegal
- abolitionist
- fugitive
- autobiography

Mary Jane Dilworth: Teacher

- polygamy
- Continental Divide
- Mormons
- missionary
- site
- cemetery

Orion Howe: Civil War Drummer Boy

- Union
- fifer
- cartridges
- Confederate
- regiment
- ammunition
- musket
- inspired
- caliber
- fife
- reveille
- desperate

Shirley Temple: Actress

- Depression
- gymnastics
- spunky
- tutored
- economy
- spoof
- immortal
- delegate
- challenging
- protocol
- irresistible
- ambassador
- studio
- bankrupt
- isolated
- despair

Melba Pattillo: Civil Rights Activist

- segregation
- equality
- lynch
- integration
- expelled
- crinoline
- spiritual
- abuse
- dignity
- barriers

S.E. Hinton: Author

- realistic
- structure
- idealism
- viewpoint
- character
- rival
- plot
- violence
- category

Midori: Violinist

- rehearse
- rehearsals
- correspondence
- recital
- ovation
- scholarship
- prodigy
- violinist
- legendary
- debut
- symphony
- concertmaster

Ryan White: AIDS Spokesperson

- AIDS
- saliva
- discrimination
- transfusion
- contaminated
- hypodermic
- hemophilia
- compassion
- virus

Trevor Ferrell: Activist for the Homeless

- suburban
- donation
- commendation
- persistent
- campaign
- grate
- volunteer
- dyslexia
- commitment

Samantha Smith: Ambassador

- ambassador
- interview
- alliance
- keynote
- communist
- exchange student
- nuclear
- communism

Oscar De La Hoya: Boxer

- barrio
- graffiti
- discipline
- Olympics
- dedication
- sparring
- amateur
- inspiration
- architecture
- seamstress

Tiger Woods: Golfer

- exaggeration
- golf clinic
- tournament
- endorsement
- foundation

Jason Gaes: Cancer Survivor

- cancer
- radiation
- lymph system
- malignant
- chemotherapy
- Burkitt's lymphoma
- tumor
- translated
- benign

Answers

BENJAMIN WEST: ARTIST

Remembering the Facts

1. 10 miles outside Philadelphia on October 19, 1738
2. He was bound for greatness.
3. his baby nephew
4. Quakers frowned on drawings, especially of people.
5. He used cat hair and a quill.
6. The books introduced him to classical painting.
7. It was his first historical painting, a new style of painting he would later make popular.
8. He wanted to study with famous painters there.
9. "historical painter to the king"
10. They showed people dressed correctly for their time, rather than in classical dress.

Understanding the Story

Answers will vary.

11. If his parents had been strict Quakers, they would not have allowed him to draw. Quakers did not allow drawings, especially of people. Drawing was seen as sinful. His talent

might have been squelched. Or he may have continued to draw against their wishes.

12. Life in the early colonies was hard. People needed all their energy just to make a living. Art was seen as a frill. People did not have time for extras.

Getting the Main Idea

He was the first world-famous artist born in America. He gained much of his fame while still in his teens and living in America. He trained many young American artists who later became famous.

Applying What You've Learned

With training, a person learns to develop the skill he or she has. A person can learn how to use color, line, and shading. Techniques can be taught. A person can learn how to use different materials to get different effects.

PHILLIS WHEATLEY: POET

Remembering the Facts

1. about 1753 in West Africa

2. Mary and Nathaniel Wheatley taught her to read the Bible, speak English and read Latin.

3. Phillis was invited to read her poetry at parties at the homes of wealthy Bostonians.

4. He did not believe a black slave could be the author.

5. The Countess of Huntingdon spread the word among her friends.

6. Poems on Various Subjects, Religious and Moral

7. She sent George Washington a poem she had written in his honor. Washington asked to meet her.

8. During the war, times were hard. People lost their jobs and homes. Phillis's husband went to debtors' prison. She was unable to sell her poetry and had no way to support herself.

Understanding the Story

9. Many families did not treat their slaves kindly. The slaves had to work hard and had few comforts. The Wheatleys treated Phillis well. They encouraged her talent and helped her reach her potential. They were proud of her achievements.

10. People do not have time to enjoy the arts during wartime. They are faced with a daily struggle to survive. Because of the war, people had no time for listening to poetry and no money for buying books of poems. Phillis had no market for her talent.

Getting the Main Idea

She was the first African American to publish a book. Her poems were equal in quality to any being written at the time. At the time many people believed that black people were less intelligent than white people. Women were also believed to be inferior to men. Phillis Wheatley's poetry shows that she had a mind equal to any man, of any race.

Applying What You've Learned

Answers will vary.

MARIA MITCHELL: ASTRONOMER

Remembering the Facts

1. lamp oil
2. The sailors used them as a guide.
3. a ship's clock
4. the height of the stars
5. It involved much rote memory of boring, moralistic lessons that the children did not understand.
6. Her mother stocked the house with books. Her father taught her to observe nature and the stars.
7. Her students were of different races. Some were rich, others poor. She used a teaching method based on observation.

8. a new comet

9. Vassar College

10. She founded the Association for the Advancement of Women. She worked for equal pay and equal rights for women.

Understanding the Story

Answers will vary.

11. Her father taught her careful observation and recording of data. Her mother taught her the love of reading. Reverend Pierce taught her that everything must be exactly right. Her Quaker heritage taught her discipline. She was self-disciplined and learned much on her own.

12. In order to succeed, one must work hard and not give up. A person who is brilliant but doesn't stick with anything will not succeed.

Getting the Main Idea

In the 1800's very few women were scientists. It was generally believed that women did not have the ability for that sort of work. Maria Mitchell proved them wrong. By the age of 12, she had shown that she could do complex math. Later, as a teacher at Vassar, she helped other young women enter the science field.

Applying What You've Learned

Quaker children had no playthings. They took pleasure in the world of nature around them. They had few distractions. They learned to watch and listen to their world.

ALLEN JAY: UNDERGROUND RAILROAD "CONDUCTOR"

Remembering the Facts

1. It was a network of people who helped slaves escape.

2. The "conductor" led the slaves from one station to another.

3. being captured and sent back into slavery

4. It stated that slave hunters or slave owners could come into the free states of the North to capture and return a slave to slavery.

5. Their religion taught them that all men are equal; therefore, one cannot be master over another.

6. Quakers did not believe in lying. Therefore, if Allen helped the man, his father could truthfully say he hadn't seen him.

7. He reached Canada safely.

8. (any two)

   (a) He was a traveling Quaker preacher.
   (b) He was a teacher.
   (c) He was a fund-raiser for Quaker colleges.

9. After the Civil War ended, all the slaves were freed. So there was no need for them to escape anymore.

10. 60,000

Understanding the Story

Answers will vary.

11. Many people put their lives at risk to help the slaves escape. If the secret route became common knowledge, those people would have been in danger.

12. Many people believed strongly that slavery was wrong. They knew many slaves were treated badly and wanted to help.

Getting the Main Idea

Some slaves were treated well. Others lived in terrible conditions or had masters who mistreated them. Those in good situations were probably less likely to run away. It also depended on the personality of the slave. Some were content with their situations; others hated being enslaved. Some may have feared the dangers of the road even more than they feared enslavement.

Applying What You've Learned

Answers will vary. Students might tell of being chased by dogs, meeting wild animals, or seeing their master looking for them, etc.

MARY JANE DILWORTH: TEACHER

Remembering the Facts

1. They did not like the Mormons' religious beliefs, especially their practice of polygamy.

2. Nauvoo

3. Brigham Young

4. When the weather became rainy, the children were cooped up inside the wagons. Mary Jane decided to play school with them to entertain them.

5. Council Bluffs, Iowa

6. He asked her to set up a school.

7. The school was in a tent set up in a corner of the square inside the fort at Salt Lake City.

8. She felt the children would remember best if they went over and over the material.

9. Hawaii

10. Mary Jane Dilworth Elementary School

Understanding the Story

Answers will vary.

11. The elementary school day is still mostly devoted to reading, writing, and arithmetic. Public schools would not include study of the Bible. Today's schools would include a wider variety of subjects such as science, social studies, and physical education.

12. A teacher should enjoy being around young people. A teacher should be enthusiastic, patient, and dedicated to the job. Mary Jane loved teaching children. She did her job faithfully with no pay just because she enjoyed doing it.

Getting the Main Idea

There were no schools on the wagon train or in the new territory of Utah. While still a teenager, Mary Jane saw the value of education and saw to it that the children were taught. By teaching, she expressed her deep devotion to God.

Applying What You've Learned

Answers will vary. Students should explain how they would schedule time for reading, math, and spelling. They should think of other activities to fill the time, such as studying nature (outside), devising educational games to teach times tables, spelling, and other subjects.

ORION HOWE: CIVIL WAR DRUMMER BOY

Remembering the Facts

1. Both sides were desperate for soldiers. They did not really check on claims of age.

2. powder monkeys, musicians (drummers or fifers)

3. to communicate the officers' orders and to keep up the morale of the troops

4. His younger brother was off with the army. Most of the boys from the school had joined the army. He felt he was missing out.

5. 55th Illinois Regiment

6. It was the key to the control of the Mississippi River. Its capture would complete the Union's encirclement of the Confederacy.

7. The city sat on a bluff overlooking the river. It was heavily armed and would be nearly impossible to attack from that side.

8. He wanted to help those who were wounded.

9. He collected cartridges from the wounded or dead. He ran under heavy fire to the supply wagons in the rear.

10. the Medal of Honor

Understanding the Story

Answers will vary.

11. At that time, it was not unusual for teens to leave school to work. It was not expected that they graduate from high school. People grew up a lot faster. The boys did not want to be left out of what they saw as a great adventure. They did not really understand what they were getting into.

12. Life in school must have seemed boring after all that he'd done. The Naval Academy had strict rules. A boy would be punished for even small misdeeds. Order and rules were important. Orion could not see the importance of those things. He was not that ready to settle down.

Getting the Main Idea

He was a hero because he risked his life many times to help others who were wounded. He collected cartridges under fire to help the soldiers. He volunteered for the dangerous mission of getting more ammunition. The fact that he was so very young made his actions even more heroic. Grown men felt they could not show less courage than this boy.

Applying What You've Learned

Answers will vary. Students may tell about a day in camp or in a battle.

SHIRLEY TEMPLE: ACTRESS

Remembering the Facts

1. It was an extreme slowdown of the American economy. People lost their jobs, savings, and homes.

2. $1\frac{1}{2}$ years (one year is acceptable)

3. *Baby Burlesks*

4. It was used for "time out" for misbehavior.

5. She could learn lines and dance steps quickly. Most of her scenes could be correctly filmed in one "take" (try).

6. *Stand Up and Cheer*

7. a miniature Academy Award (Oscar)

8. She was isolated from other children. She was kept under armed guard for her protection. She didn't go to school until seventh grade.

9. Everyone wanted to remember her as a child.

10. politics

Understanding the Story

Answers will vary.

11. She was a brave, spunky girl. She was so cute and full of energy. People seeing her couldn't help but smile.

12. No. If a star is wildly popular like Shirley, a normal life is impossible. People want to get close to the star. They won't leave the star alone.

Getting the Main Idea

A fine piece of art (music, film, painting, etc.) draws us in. For a time we become a part of it, and it a part of us. It makes us forget our everyday cares for a while. It pleases our mind and soul.

Applying What You've Learned

Any reasonable answer is acceptable. It could be a star of film, music, or sports.

MELBA PATTILLO: CIVIL RIGHTS ACTIVIST

Remembering the Facts

1. Segregation is the separation of one racial group from another.

2. The court ruled that segregated schools were not equal. Schools should be integrated.

3. She taught her to rely on the teachings of the Bible.

4. He sent the Arkansas National Guard to keep the black students from entering the school.

5. He sent the 101st Airborne Division to force the governor to allow the students into school.

6. when the troops withdrew from the halls

7. Governor Faubus ordered the high schools closed. Some white people were so furious that the lives of the black students were in danger. The students were sent out of state.

8. *Warriors Don't Cry*

9. Her memories of the past were too painful.

10. They were cheered. Fans wanted their autographs. Governor Bill Clinton welcomed them. The black student-body president of Central High School welcomed them.

Understanding the Story

Answers will vary.

11. The actions of the Little Rock Nine made much of the white community angry. They took out their anger on all black people. Black people had learned over the years that it was easier to give in than to rock the boat.

12. They probably looked for high-achieving students who were strong and mature for their age. The students would have to be able to withstand a lot of pressure.

Getting the Main Idea

It was a very visible struggle. It was shown nightly on the television news and in the newspapers. It was an epic struggle of good (the innocent children) versus evil (Governor Faubus and the Arkansas National Guard).

Applying What You've Learned

The times of day that are less easily controlled by teachers would be hardest. Changing classes in a crowded hallway would be an easy time for students to bother each other. Teachers cannot watch an entire cafeteria. P.E. classes are large and usually involved taking showers and changing clothes. The best times would be inside a classroom.

S.E. HINTON: AUTHOR

Remembering the Facts

1. In Tulsa, Oklahoma, in 1950.

2. the Socs (socials) and the Greasers
3. They didn't like the fact that gangs, drugs, and violence were shown in the book.
4. The story is told from the viewpoint of a teen-age boy. She was afraid boys would not read the book if they knew the author was a girl.
5. She got writer's block.
6. (any two) *That Was Then, This Is Now; Rumble Fish; Tex; Taming the Star Runner; Big David, Little David; The Puppy Sister*
7. Read a lot. Then practice writing. Write for yourself.
8. Teens are in a state of rapid change. Their ideals are tested and they must learn to compromise. They are more interesting to her than adults are.
9. middle school and high school
10. young adult literature

Understanding the Story

11. The author understands what it is like to be a teen. She shows their world as it is. She doesn't talk down to them or show a sugar-coated world.
12. She liked to play with boys more than girls. So she grew to understand how boys think. She loved to read. By reading, she learned how to write well.

Getting the Main Idea

Young adult literature shows teenage characters dealing with real problems. Reading the stories of how other teens deal with their problems can help students learn things about themselves and how they can solve their own problems. It also shows them that they are not alone in the way they feel.

Applying What You've Learned

Answers will vary. Caution students not to describe a person they know. The character should be fictional.

MIDORI: VIOLINIST

Remembering the Facts

1. Her mother was a professional violinist, and Midori loved to listen to her.

2. her mother

3. A friend of Midori's mother made a tape of Midori playing and took it to Dorothy Delay.

4. Aspen Music Festival

5. so Midori could attend Juilliard Music School

6. The E-string on two violins broke as she was performing a difficult solo. She handled the situation calmly, with grace.

7. Arts education had been cut from the New York City public schools. Midori wanted children to have the chance to hear good music as she did when she was growing up.

8. presents a series of free concerts for school children; sponsors an instrumental instruction program; presents after-school programs for parents and children

Understanding the Story

Answers will vary.

9. He did not want Midori to get "burned out." He preferred her to have a few, carefully chosen experiences. He wanted her to work on expanding her repertoire and perfecting her skills.

10. They lack the ability to continue to focus on practicing long hours over the years. They "burn out" on music. They have the talent, but lack the dedication, drive, or love of music needed to make a lifetime of music performance.

Getting the Main Idea

A well-rounded person should study a variety of subjects. The arts teach skills different from those learned through arithmetic or spelling. The arts add joy and beauty to our lives. Research indicates that skill in one of the arts can improve children's success in the classroom as well.

Applying What You've Learned

Answers will vary. It could be a concert, trip to an art museum, a class, etc.

RYAN WHITE: AIDS SPOKESPERSON

Remembering the Facts

1. 1981

2. He was a hemophiliac. He needed blood with extra clotting factor so his cuts could heal normally.

3. (any order) through sexual contact; by sharing contaminated needles; by blood transfusions with contaminated blood

4. They did not understand how AIDS is spread. They knew AIDS is fatal. They did not want their children to get it.

5. He dated. He liked music and cars. He had a job.

6. He knew he could help other young people with AIDS.

7. It provides money for medical expenses of people with AIDS.

8. (any two) He changed people's views toward AIDS victims. He taught people the facts about AIDS. He was an example of courage in the face of illness and discrimination.

Understanding the Story

Answers will vary.

9. The big difference was education. The school leaders in Cicero made sure each student and parent at the high school learned the facts about AIDS. The leaders wanted Ryan to be accepted. They worked hard to make that happen.

10. Ryan was treated unjustly because of his illness. He was teased and threatened. No one would have anything to do with him. Many minority groups have suffered in these same ways.

Getting the Main Idea

Ryan White was able to educate people about AIDS. When people understood more about the disease, they were not as afraid. They were able to reach out in compassion to help other victims.

Applying What You've Learned

Answers will vary. Students should talk about feeling some fear, or at least mixed emotions.

TREVOR FERRELL: ACTIVIST FOR THE HOMELESS

Remembering the Facts

1. He saw a story on television about the homeless.
2. He convinced his parents to take him downtown to give his blanket and pillow to a homeless person.
3. Dyslexia is a reading disability.
4. He put up posters. He put an ad in the newspaper.
5. His story appeared in the local newspaper. Then it was picked up by TV stations and large newspapers.
6. They teased him about what he was doing.
7. The Peace Mission Movement donated an old hotel.
8. (any two) Mr. Ferrell had to close his repair shop. Mrs. Ferrell was tired from hard work. Trevor began to fall behind in school.
9. He accepted them as people. He did not judge them.
10. (any one) a commendation from President Reagan; the John Rogers Integrity Award; a resolution passed by the city council

Understanding the Story

Answers will vary.

11. There are many reasons. Some examples: substance abuse; mental illness; broken family ties; poverty; loss of unskilled jobs; urban renewal, which forces people out of buildings

that are renovated and put in a higher rent category. Some choose to be homeless because they reject society's norms.

12. Volunteering makes people feel good about themselves. It is a way to get one's own problems in perspective. It allows people to appreciate the good things they have. It helps them see the good in other people. It is a way to feel as if you are making a difference in the world.

Getting the Main Idea

We learn that one person really can make a difference. An 11-year-old boy was the inspiration for hundreds of people. If we think we cannot make a difference, we won't. If each person took on a simple task where they live, a lot of society's problems would be lessened.

Applying What You've Learned

Answers will vary. Some things to do might include finding out what is being done in your area and offer to help; collect food for shelters; volunteer to cook food; collect clothing for the needy; collect household items like blankets, sleeping bags, and pillows; donate money. Your efforts not only help needy people, they may inspire others to volunteer as well.

SAMANTHA SMITH: AMBASSADOR

Remembering the Facts

1. mid-1940's (post-WWII) to the end of the 1980's
2. The U.S. and the Soviet Union tried to stockpile more and larger nuclear weapons.
3. She was afraid of nuclear war.
4. They said she was only 10, so she couldn't be expected to understand what the Soviet people were like.
5. She wrote to the Soviet ambassador to the United States.
6. He explained that the Soviets, too, wanted peace. He invited her to visit to see what they were like.
7. their clothes and music

8. She wrote a book. She gave interviews on television and for newspapers.

9. (any two) A flower, a star, and a children's center were named after her.

10. to sponsor exchange students between the U.S. and former parts of the Soviet Union

Understanding the Story

Answers will vary.

11. Even though she was so young, Samantha acted on her beliefs. In doing so, she was able to achieve more for world peace than anyone would have believed.

12. Yes. People admired the spunky girl who had dared to write a letter to the Soviet leader Andropov. She charmed people in both countries with her winning smile. Because of her youth she could relate easily to Soviet children.

Getting the Main Idea

Yes. People around the world were fascinated with her trip. She made people realize (if only for a while) that we are more alike than different.

Applying What You've Learned

Samantha would have been concerned with any "hot spot" in the world or any area where children are suffering. Any answer along these lines is acceptable.

OSCAR DE LA HOYA: BOXER

Remembering the Facts

1. East Los Angeles
2. He was getting beaten up because he was not in a gang.
3. Paul Gonzales
4. dedication, discipline, and desire
5. He had a tutor.
6. She hoped he would win an Olympic gold medal.

7. He won an Olympic gold medal in the 132-pound weight class.

8. WBC (World Boxing Council) super-lightweight champion

9. (any two) renovated a gym for youth; donated money to Garfield students for scholarships; donated money to the school for activities

10. pursue a degree in architecture

Understanding the Story

Answers will vary.

11. Differences: He is not loud or boastful about his wins. He is polite and well-mannered. Same: He loves to fight. He trains hard.

12. A gang gives kids a sense of identity. It is a group of other kids who will stick by you no matter what. It may give kids a feeling of security to be part of a group. Also, many kids grow up expecting to be in a gang, because it is part of their environment. They may have little or no supervision from home, so the gang takes the place of the family.

Getting the Main Idea

Oscar De La Hoya is a role model because he set goals for himself and worked hard to make them happen. He was not taken in by the false glamour of the gangs. He set his own course and stuck to it. Now that he has achieved his goals and some wealth, he is trying to help others who still live in East L.A. by building a gym that can be a safe haven and by providing scholarships.

Applying What You've Learned

To resist the gangs, you would need to find other activities to become involved in. School, church, or family activities would fill this need. You would have to try to avoid areas where gangs met. You would need to make friends with other kids who were not in gangs. It would take great strength to set your course and stick to it.

TIGER WOODS: GOLFER

Remembering the Facts

1. (any order) He is a superstar of his sport. He creates a lot of excitement for his sport.

2. six months

3. At two, he appeared on *The Mike Douglas Show* and bested Bob Hope at putting. Later that year, he appeared on *That's Incredible.*

4. Earl Woods's commander in Vietnam was a "tiger" on the battlefield. Eldrick played like a tiger on the golf course. So Earl named him Tiger.

5. His father put him through a "boot camp" to toughen him up when he was 11. His mother taught him the principles of Buddhism.

6. the U.S. Junior Amateur championship

7. the U.S. Amateur championship

8. the Master's Tournament

9. endorsements (advertising)

10. He is sponsoring golf clinics for minority young people.

Understanding the Story

Answers will vary.

11. Many people look up to him. They expect him to be perfect and a role model at all times. This puts extra pressure on him to succeed in golf. Also, he must be careful about what he says and does in public.

12. determination, patience, focus on one's goals, desire to win, willingness to practice over long periods of time, etc.

Getting the Main Idea

He has excelled by hard work and determination. He has a winning attitude. His positive outlook helps him overcome obstacles. He is polite and cheerful. He wants to use his position to help other kids succeed.

Applying What You've Learned

Students could mention keeping a positive attitude, ignoring racist slights, winning more tournaments, keeping the desire to win, avoiding "burn-out," etc.

JASON GAES: CANCER SURVIVOR

Remembering the Facts

1. A small black tumor appeared in his mouth.

2. It is a mass of cancer cells.

3. Burkitt's lymphoma

4. It beams high-energy X-rays at the cancer cells, damaging or destroying them.

5. The chemicals go through the entire body via the blood-stream to kill cancer cells that may have spread.

6. He read a book in which the boy with cancer died. He wanted to write a book about a boy who lived.

7. He wanted some good to come from what he had endured. He talked about what to expect and how to cope.

8. A publisher saw a TV program about Jason. He wanted to publish the book to help other children.

9. *You Don't Have to Die*

10. He appeared on talk shows, gave magazine interviews, traveled the country giving speeches, and answered letters and phone calls.

Understanding the Story

Answers will vary.

11. Everyone would be tired and stressed. Other children might feel they weren't getting enough attention. The parents might disagree about treatment. Bills would mount.

12. Agree: She is right that any family faced with a health crisis must try their best to deal with it. Disagree: This family is heroic in that it showed unusual strength and courage.

Their unselfish attitude helped others suffering as they were.

Getting the Main Idea

Jason could speak on their level. He knew what things would bother a child more than an adult would. He knew how to explain things so a child would understand. Young children do not need a lot of detailed information. Jason gave them the amount of information they might need on a level they could relate to. Also, his survival would give them hope.

Applying What You've Learned

Answers will vary. The situation about which students write would not necessarily need to be a huge crisis, just any problem they were able to handle.

Additional Activities

Benjamin West: Artist

1. Go to an art museum to see a collection of paintings. Write a paragraph about the visit.

2. Read more about the life of Benjamin West.

3. Find photographs of Benjamin West's paintings in an art book or in one of his biographies.

4. Find out how a person who wants a career in art might get training to be an artist.

5. Read more about one of the famous American artists trained by Benjamin West: Samuel F. Morse, Gilbert Stuart, John Trumbull, Charles Willson Peale, Rembrandt Peale, John Copley, Thomas Sully, or Washington Allston.

6. Find out more information about the Royal Academy of Arts, of which Benjamin West was a charter member.

Phillis Wheatley: Poet

1. Read some of Phillis Wheatley's poetry.

2. Find out more about the slave ships that brought Africans to America.

3. Read more about the events of the Revolutionary War taking place in Boston where Phillis lived. Examples: the Stamp Act, the Boston Tea Party, etc.

4. Find out more about George Whitefield, an evangelist in the religious revival movement called the Great Awakening during the 18th century.

Maria Mitchell: Astronomer

1. Find out more about a ship's chronometer. Learn how it is used to find longitude at sea.
2. Find out more about a sextant and how it works. Sextants are used to measure the altitude of a star in order to determine longitude.
3. Look up more information about Nantucket Island—its climate, customs, and people.
4. Read about the days of the whaling ships.
5. Find out about whaling today.
6. Find out more about the Quakers and their beliefs.

Allen Jay: Underground Railroad "Conductor"

1. Read more about the Underground Railroad. One book you might read is *North Star to Freedom* by Gena Gorrell (1997).
2. Read about the life of Harriet Tubman, the most famous African American "conductor" on the Underground Railroad.
3. Read the Thirteenth Amendment to the United States Constitution. Discuss its provisions.
4. Read more about the history of slavery in America.
5. Read more about one of these famous figures who were involved in this period of black history: Nat Turner, Harriet Tubman, Frederick Douglass, Thomas Garrett, William Lloyd Garrison, Sojourner Truth, Harriet Beecher Stowe, John Brown.

Mary Jane Dilworth: Teacher

1. Read more about the life of the Mormon leader, Brigham Young.
2. Find out more about the state of Utah.

3. Read more about the Mormon trek west to settle the Great Salt Lake valley.

4. Locate an example of an old speller or other old textbook. Report to the class on how it differs from books used today.

Orion Howe: Civil War Drummer Boy

1. Read about another famous Civil War drummer boy, Johnny Clem. He was a Union drummer in the battle of Shiloh in April 1862. When his drum was shattered by a shell, 12-year-old Johnny grabbed a musket and started shooting back. He became known as "Johnny Shiloh." A year later he fought in the Battle of Chickamauga. His heroics in that battle earned him the name "The Drummer Boy of Chickamauga."

2. Find out more about the Battle of Vicksburg. Report on it to the class.

3. For more details about Orion Howe's life, read *The Drummer Boy of Vicksburg* by G. Clifton Wisler.

Shirley Temple: Actress

1. Read Shirley Temple's autobiography, *Child Star*.

2. View one of Shirley Temple's movies. A few of the best known include:

> *Little Miss Marker* (1934)
> *The Little Colonel* (1935)
> *The Littlest Rebel* (1935)
> *Captain January* (1936)
> *Poor Little Rich Girl* (1936)
> *Stowaway* (1936)
> *Wee Willie Winkie* (1937)
> *Heidi* (1937)
> *Rebecca of Sunnybrook Farm* (1938)
> *Little Miss Broadway* (1938)
> *The Little Princess* (1939)

(There are many others.)

3. Find out more about the Great Depression.

Melba Pattillo: Civil Rights Activist

1. Read Melba's account of the integration of Central High School in *Warriors Don't Cry*.

2. Read the book *Freedom's Children* by Ellen Levine. It tells the stories of 30 teenagers during the civil rights movement in the South.

3. Find out more about some of the people and events of the civil rights movement:

   > Emmett Till, killed for talking "improperly" to a white woman.
   > the Montgomery Bus Boycott
   > *Brown* v. *Board of Education of Topeka*
   > the church bombing in Birmingham, AL, which killed four girls
   > "Bloody Sunday" and the Selma-to-Montgomery march
   > Voting Rights Act of 1965
   > Jim Crow laws

   Choose a topic that interests you and report on it to the class. Use the list above or choose another civil rights topic.

S.E. Hinton: Author

1. Read one of S.E. Hinton's books. Report on it to the class. Her books are:

   > *The Outsiders*, 1967
   > *That Was Then, This is Now*, 1971
   > *Rumble Fish*, 1975
   > *Tex*, 1979
   > *Taming the Star Runner*, 1988
   > *Big David, Little David*, 1994
   > *The Puppy Sister*, 1995

2. Read Jay Daly's biography of S.E. Hinton, *Presenting S.E. Hinton*.

3. View the 1982 movie *The Outsiders*, starring Matt Dillon, Rob Lowe, Tom Cruise, Emilio Estevez, and Patrick Swayze.

4. Other writers following S.E. Hinton's style include Paul Zindel, Richard Peck, M.E. Kerr, Paula Danziger, and Robert

Cormier. Check out one of their books at the library. Compare their style to S.E. Hinton's.

Midori: Violinist

1. Obtain and listen to a recording of one of Midori's performances.

2. Read about another famous violinist such as Isaac Stern or Pinchas Zukerman. Another famous very young violinist is Sarah Chang.

3. Find out more about Midori and Friends. Look on the web at http://www.midoriandfriends.org/adventur.htm

4. Read a recent article to find out what Midori is doing with her career now.

Ryan White: AIDS Spokesperson

1. Find out more about hemophilia.

2. Read the latest information in the fight against AIDS. Call the National AIDS Hotline (1-800-342-AIDS) or the National AIDS Clearinghouse (1-800-458-5231).

3. Read about the work of David Ho, a scientist who studies AIDS. You can read about him in the book *16 Extraordinary Asian Americans* (J. Weston Walch, Publisher).

4. View the program *I Have AIDS—A Teenager's Story*. This is available from:

    The National AIDS Information Clearinghouse
    P.O. Box 6003, Dept. G
    Rockville, MD 20850
    1-800-458-5231

5. View *The Ryan White Story*, a television movie about Ryan.

6. Read Ryan's autobiography, *Ryan White: My Own Story*.

Trevor Ferrell: Activist for the Homeless

1. Imagine that you are suddenly homeless. Write a paragraph telling what you think your thoughts would be. Tell where you might go for help.

2. Find out what agencies in your town work with the homeless and needy citizens.

3. Invite a representative from an agency that works with the needy in your town to speak to your class, explaining the work of the agency. Ask how individuals can help with this work.

4. Some of the homeless are homeless by choice. Discuss how this could be. Why might some of the homeless resist help?

5. Look for stories about homelessness or other social problems in your community in the newspaper. Discuss these in class.

Samantha Smith: Ambassador

1. Find out more information about the Samantha Smith Foundation.

2. Read more about some of the major events in the Cold War. Some interesting topics might include the Iron Curtain, the Berlin Wall, the Truman Doctrine, or the Bay of Pigs Crisis.

3. Read Samantha's book, *Journey to the Soviet Union*. It is short, interesting, and filled with beautiful photographs.

4. Read more about Yuri Andropov, the Soviet leader.

Oscar De La Hoya: Boxer

1. Find out what Oscar De La Hoya is doing today.

2. Read the stories of other famous boxers, such as Muhammad Ali or Sugar Ray Leonard.

3. Find out the rules for a WBC boxing match.

Tiger Woods: Golfer

1. A large number of biographies of Tiger Woods were written in 1997. Obtain one of these at the library and read it. Report to the class any additional things you learn about Tiger Woods.

2. Read about another famous pro golfer. Examples: Arnold Palmer, Jack Nicklaus, Nancy Lopez, Ben Hogan.

3. Find out more information about the Master's Tournament.

4. Find out what Tiger Woods is doing now.

5. Play a game of golf. If you don't have clubs, you can rent them at your local public golf course. Report to the class on your reaction to the game.

Jason Gaes: Cancer Survivor

1. Obtain a copy of Jason's book and read it.

2. Choose a type of cancer and present a report on it to the class.

3. Invite a speaker from the American Cancer Society, Leukemia Society, or a pediatric oncologist (a doctor who treats cancer) to speak to your class about childhood cancer.

4. For more information about cancer, call the American Cancer Society at 1-800-ACS-2345.

5. The following groups publish many helpful pamphlets on various topics. Write for information:

American Cancer Society
1599 Clifton Road, N.E.
Atlanta, GA 30329

Cancer Information Service
Office of Cancer Communications
Building 31, Room 10A24
Bethesda, MD 20893-3100

Leukemia Society of America
733 Third Avenue
New York, NY 10017

References

Benjamin West: Artist

Abrams, Ann Uhry. *The Valiant Hero: Benjamin West and Grand-Style History Painting.* Washington, D.C.: Smithsonian Institution Press, 1985.

Alberts, Robert C. *Benjamin West: A Biography.* Boston: Houghton-Mifflin Co., 1978.

Flexner, James Thomas. *America's Old Masters: First Artists of the New World.* New York: The Viking Press, 1939.

Phillis Wheatley: Poet

Richmond, Merle. *Phillis Wheatley, Poet.* New York: Chelsea House Publishers, 1988.

Sherrow, Victoria. *Phillis Wheatley.* Chelsea House Publishers, 1992.

Shields, John C. "Phillis Wheatley." *Black Women in America, An Historical Encyclopedia.* Darlene Clark, ed. New York: Carlson Publishing, Inc., 1993, pages 1251–1255.

Shields, John C. "Phillis Wheatley." *Notable Black American Women.*

Jessie Carrey Smith, ed. Detroit: Gale Research, 1992, pages 1243–1248.

Maria Mitchell: Astronomer

Brill, Marlene Targ. *Extraordinary Young People.* New York: Children's Press, 1996, pages 46–49.

Carmer, Carl. *A Cavalcade of Young Americans.* New York: Lothrop, Lee & Shepard Co., Inc., 1958, pages 133–139.

Gormaly, Beatrice. *Maria Mitchell: The Soul of an Astronomer.* Grand Rapids, MI: W.B. Eerdmans, 1995.

Wright, Helen. *Sweeper in the Sky.* New York: Macmillan Company, 1949.

Allen Jay: Underground Railroad "Conductor"

Carmer, Carl. *A Cavalcade of Young Americans.* New York: Lothrop, Lee & Shepard Co., Inc., 1958, pages 160–168.

Gorrell, Gena K. *North Star to Freedom: The Story of the Underground*

Railroad. New York: Delacorte Press, 1996.

Jay, Allen. *The Autobiography of Allen Jay.* Philadelphia: The John C. Winston Co., 1908.

Drew, Benjamin. *A North-Side View of Slavery.* Boston, 1856.

Mary Jane Dilworth: Teacher

Burt, Olive W. *Young Wayfarers of the Early West.* New York: Hawthorn Books, Inc., 1968, pages 84–102.

Fradin, Dennis Brindell. *Utah.* Chicago: Children's Press, 1994, pages 13–14.

Orion Howe: Civil War Drummer Boy

Dillon, Doug. "Boys of the Civil War." *Boys' Life*, November 1997, page 11.

King, Charles. "Boys of the Civil War Days." *The Photographic History of the Civil War.* New Jersey: The Blue and Gray Press, 1987, pages 190–196.

Wisler, G. Clifton. *The Drummer Boy of Vicksburg.* New York: Lodestar Books, an affiliate of Dutton, 1997.

Shirley Temple: Actress

Black, Shirley Temple. *Child Star: An Autobiography.* New York: McGraw-Hill, 1988.

David, Lester, and Irene Lester. *The Shirley Temple Story.* New York: G.P. Putnam's Sons, 1983.

Edwards, Anne. *Shirley Temple: American Princess.* New York: William Morrow & Co., 1988.

Melba Pattillo: Civil Rights Activist

Beals, Melba Pattillo. *Warriors Don't Cry.* New York: Pocket Books, a division of Simon & Schuster, Inc., 1994.

Levine, Ellen. *Freedom's Children.* New York: G.P. Putnam's Sons, 1993.

S.E. Hinton: Author

Daly, Jay. *Presenting S.E. Hinton.* Boston: Twayne Publishers, 1987.

"Hinton, S(usan) E(loise)." *Something About the Author*, Vol. 19. Anne Commire, ed. Detroit: Gale Research, 1980, pages 147–148.

Hinton, S.E. *The Outsiders.* New York: Viking Press, 1967.

"S(usan) E(loise) Hinton." *Children's Literature Review*, Vol. 23. Gerard J. Senick, ed. Detroit: Gale Research, 1991, pages 132–150.

Midori: Violinist

"Midori." *Current Biography Yearbook*, 1990, pp. 439–442.

"Midori." *Notable Asian Americans.* Helen Zia and Susan B. Gall, eds. New York: Gale Research, 1995, pages 254–256.

"Midori and Friends." http://www.midoriandfriends.org/midori.htm

"The Soul of a Prodigy." *Reader's Digest,* Vol. 30, March 1987, pages 84–88.

Ryan White: AIDS Spokesperson

Friedman, Jack, and Bill Shaw. "The Quiet Victories of Ryan White." *People Weekly,* May 30, 1988, pages 88–94.

"Remembering Ryan White." *Newsweek,* April 23, 1990, page 24.

Shaw, Bill. "Candle in the Wind." *People Weekly,* April 23, 1990, pages 88–90.

White, Ryan, and Ann Marie Cunningham. *Ryan White: My Own Story.* New York: Dial Books, 1991.

Trevor Ferrell: Activist for the Homeless

Ferrell, Frank, and Janet Ferrell. *Trevor's Place: The Story of the Boy Who Brings Hope to the Homeless.* San Francisco: Harper & Row Publishers, 1985.

Plummer, William. "Philadelphia's Street People Have Found a Ministering Angel in Tiny Trevor Ferrell." *People Weekly,* March 26, 1984.

Samantha Smith: Ambassador

Martin, Patricia Stone. *Samantha Smith: Young Ambassador.* Vero Beach, FL.: Rourke Enterprises, 1987.

Smith, Arthur, and Samantha Smith. *Samantha Smith: Journey to the Soviet Union.* Boston: Little, Brown & Co., 1985.

Oscar De La Hoya: Boxer

Kriegel, Mark. "The Great (Almost) White Hope." *Esquire,* Vol. 126, No. 5, November 1996, pages 81–86.

"Oscar De La Hoya." *Current Biography,* Vol. 58, No. 1, January 1997.

Tresniowski, Alex. "Moving on Up." *People Weekly,* Vol. 47, No. 2, January 20, 1997, pages 93–94.

Tiger Woods: Golfer

Andrisani, John. *The Tiger Woods Way.* New York: Crown Publishers, Inc., 1997.

Mark, Steve. "Golf is Cool." *Boys' Life,* August 1997, pages 6–7.

Spiegel, Peter. "Jordan & Co: Sports Top 40." *Forbes,* Vol. 160, No. 13, December 15, 1997, pages 180–206.

"Tiger Woods." *Current Biography Yearbook,* November 1997.

Tresniowski, Alex. "Eyes on the Tiger." *People Weekly,* Vol. 47, No. 16, April 28, 1997, pages 89–92.

Jason Gaes: Cancer Survivor

Gaes, Jason. *My book for kids with cansur.* Aberdeen, SD: Melius & Peterson Publishing, 1987.

Gaes, Geralyn, and Craig Gaes, with Philip Bashe. *You Don't Have to Die: One Family's Guide to Surviving Childhood Cancer.* New York: Villard Books, 1992.